"In our increasingly unchurched culture, wonderfully committed pastors are entering church ministry without significant background in the daily life and practices of the local church. With warmth and maturity, reflecting his years of pastoring and training pastors, Charlie Wingard provides this helpful primer on how to go about the care of souls, the duties of a pastor, and the loving rigors of organizing and leading local church practices, services, and people."

— **Bryan Chapell**, Pastor, Grace Presbyterian Church, Peoria, Illinois; President Emeritus, Covenant Theological Seminary; Author, *Christ-Centered Preaching*

"Charlie Wingard was my pastor during my seminary years. I learned from him then, and I am still learning from him today. This book is simply excellent—extremely practical and exceedingly wise. The writing is clear, direct, and full of good sense, just as I would expect from Pastor Wingard."

— **Kevin DeYoung**, Senior Pastor, Christ Covenant Church, Matthews, North Carolina; Assistant Professor of Systematic Theology, Reformed Theological Seminary, Charlotte

"Charlie Wingard is the consummate Reformed pastor. I watch with something akin to astonishment as I see him ministering (seemingly ubiquitously) to our students at Reformed Theological Seminary and to his flock at First Presbyterian Church. I cannot conceive of anyone from whom I would rather receive counsel on the practice of the Christian ministry. Needless to say, then, I am thrilled that he has written *Help for the New Pastor*. Even if you have been in the ministry for a long time, there are things to be learned and relearned here. I have. You will, too."

— **Ligon Duncan**, Chancellor and CEO, Reformed Theological Seminary

"Charlie Wingard is a pastor's pastor. He understands the range of demands that insist upon his time and press upon his mind. He knows the degree to which a pastor must continually be growing in emotional, spiritual, and theological intelligence. He understands that to be useful, the pastor must love people and must highly prize the church of God while at the same time developing his own life with God. All this could easily overwhelm us, but Charlie helps us to negotiate these competing pressures and to emerge with an even stronger conviction that to be a minister of the gospel is the highest and noblest of callings."

—**Liam Goligher**, Senior Minister, Tenth Presbyterian Church, Philadelphia

"This book is a treasure chest of wisdom from an experienced pastor. Charlie's love for ministers evidences itself in these pages as he provides practical and godly advice. It will save many young pastors from unnecessary error and heartache; maybe more importantly, it will save the congregations they serve from the same things. As I read *Help for the New Pastor*, I found myself thinking, 'This is as close as one can get to sitting down with a friendly, older, wiser mentor and learning at his feet, without actually doing so in person.' Take up and read, young pastors. You will find yourselves encouraged, stimulated, challenged, and equipped."

—**Jason Helopoulos**, Associate Pastor, University Reformed Church, East Lansing, Michigan; Author, *The New Pastor's Handbook: Help and Encouragement in the First Years of Ministry*

"When I was ordained in my first call, I had an experienced pastor as my mentor. As I watched him handle the range of ministry in the life of our congregation, I gained wisdom and insight that I've fallen back on time and again throughout my own ministerial life. For those who don't have the opportunity that I had, Charlie Wingard's new book does nearly the same thing. Page after page, the young pastor receives sage advice from a more experienced pastor-educator about the kinds of opportunities and challenges that happen in small to medium-sized churches. Not only will you find help in these pages, but you'll find renewed confidence and zeal for your gospel call!"

—**Sean Michael Lucas**, Senior Pastor, Independent Presbyterian Church, Memphis; Chancellor's Professor of Church History, Reformed Theological Seminary, Jackson

"A pastor's first few years in the ministry are a bit like buttoning the first button of your shirt: if you get it right, everything that follows is more likely to line up properly; but if you get it wrong, moving forward will be much more difficult. For that reason, I was glad to read *Help for the New Pastor*. It is evident from the very first chapter that Wingard has trodden the path that the young pastor wishes to tread, and he is clearly a reliable and faithful guide. The advice you will find in these pages is biblical, solid, practical, comprehensive, and specific. I look forward to incorporating it into our church's training program for young ministers."

—**Mike McKinley**, Senior Pastor, Sterling Park Baptist Church, Sterling, Virginia

"Many ministries fail or receive fatal blows in their first year of ministry. Often it's because of attempting too many things at once or failing to identify and do the basics of pastoral ministry. That's where this book will prove uniquely useful to new pastors. It cuts through the fog and confusion of the early days in a new church and lasers in on what simply must be done and how to do it well. It's just been added to the required reading list of my Ministry and Leadership class."

—**David Murray**, Professor of Old Testament and Practical Theology, Puritan Reformed Theological Seminary

"Nothing is more valuable to seminarians and young pastors than sage advice from one who has faithfully labored for decades in the vineyard of the Lord. In *Help for the New Pastor*, Charlie Wingard provides it. In this succinct and highly accessible little volume, he dispenses a flood of practical wisdom for ministry. If you are preparing for the pastorate or just starting out, carefully read and apply this book. Your (future) congregation will be grateful."

—**Jon D. Payne**, Minister, Christ Church Presbyterian (PCA), Charleston, South Carolina

"As a young seminary student in the early 1990s, I was a member of the church in which Wingard pastored. I served as his secretary, taught Sunday school, and preached my very first sermon in that church. During those formative years, I watched him preach, teach, study, disciple, visit, evangelize, suffer for, and love an ever-growing congregation. The work was not flashy or fancy. There were no gimmicks or tricks. It was simple, solid, means-of-grace gospel work. If you are preparing for ministry, are in the early stages of your ministry, or need to rethink your priorities in ministry, this book will provide you with wise counsel for your own work. It is biblical, theological, and exceptionally practical. By the end of this book, you will likely count Wingard as your friend and partner in the great work of gospel ministry."

—**Miles V. Van Pelt**, Alan Belcher Professor of Old Testament and Biblical Languages, Academic Dean, Reformed Theological Seminary, Jackson

"'Fools learn from experience. I prefer to learn from the experience of others,' Otto von Bismarck once said. From the wealth of his own experience, Charlie Wingard has provided a valuable resource for the church, an eminently practical volume for those beginning in ministry. Whether you are just starting out, have some wounds that need healing, or want to reminisce about what you now know that you wish you had known when you were younger, pick up this book. Or, even better, give it to a new pastor."

—**Rankin Wilbourne**, Pastor, Pacific Crossroads Church, Los Angeles; Author, *Union with Christ*

HELP
for the
NEW
PASTOR

Practical Advice for Your
First Year of Ministry

CHARLES MALCOLM WINGARD

P U B L I S H I N G
P.O. BOX 817 • PHILLIPSBURG • NEW JERSEY 08865-0817

ISBN: 978-1-62995-467-7 (pbk.)
ISBN: 978-1-62995-468-4 (ePub)
ISBN: 978-1-62995-469-1 (Mobi)

Printed in the United States of America

Library of Congress Cataloging-in-Publication Data

Names: Wingard, Charles Malcolm, author.
Title: Help for the new pastor : practical advice for your first year of
  ministry / Charles Malcolm Wingard.
Description: Phillipsburg : P&R Publishing, 2018. | Includes index.
Identifiers: LCCN 2017048565| ISBN 9781629954677 (pbk.) | ISBN
  9781629954684 (epub) | ISBN 9781629954691 (mobi)
Subjects: LCSH: Pastoral theology.
Classification: LCC BV4011.3 .W564 2018 | DDC 253--dc23
LC record available at https://lccn.loc.gov/2017048565

For Lynne, who fills my life and ministry
with joy, encouragement, and daily laughter.

Contents

Foreword

WHAT I WOULD have given, as a young pastor, to sit down with an esteemed, seasoned pastor and learn from him about the ministry. Well, this kind of help is exactly what *Help for the New Pastor* provides! And the pastor-mentor is Dr. Charles Wingard, a man with over three decades of hands-on pastoral experience, who has pastored churches both small and large and has seen it all—and now is Professor of Practical Theology at Reformed Theological Seminary in Jackson, Mississippi.

This book reads as if you are sitting in his study, coffee cup in hand, as he kindly answers your questions, as well as addressing some important issues that you had never dreamed of. Dr. Wingard's style is warm and genial, down-to-earth, and devoid of ecclesial pretense, though he draws not only from the Bible but from the deep wells of Reformed theology. In a nutshell, this book is unerringly wise, biblically informed, and pastoral, its common sense made crystal clear and utterly accessible.

Help for the New Pastor is laid out in eighteen concise chapters that address the day-in/day-out responsibilities of a pastor's life and advise on cultivating his interior life and disciplines. Again, the chapters are written with a smile—a serious smile. The chapters are, frankly, enjoyable to read. Though I myself have weathered many summers and winters in the ministry, this resource has provided me with many excellent thoughts for my "Pastoralia" files that will be used to enrich my students.

What a gift this book will be to those embarking on their holy call to "preach the word" (2 Tim. 4:2) and "shepherd the flock of God" (1 Peter 5:2). What pitfalls I would have avoided, and what enrichments I would have experienced, if this book had been in my hands when I began my pastoral journey.

Young pastors, *tolle lege*. Parishioners, kindly put a copy in your pastor's hand.

R. Kent Hughes
Senior Pastor Emeritus, College Church, Wheaton, Illinois
John Boyer Professor of Culture and Evangelism,
Westminster Theological Seminary

Preface

THIS BOOK BEGAN in 2011 in the mind of my wife, Lynne. She reminded me that I had served as a pastor for more than three decades and that I love working with seminary students. "So why," she asked, "don't you write a book about pastoral ministry?"

One good reason is that I'd rather do pastoral ministry than write about it. But she persisted, and this book is the fruit of her loving perseverance.

The book remained largely unwritten until 2014, when I began teaching pastoral theology at Reformed Theological Seminary in Jackson, Mississippi. What follows is, for the most part, counsel I give my students. I am primarily interested not in where they will be five, ten, or even twenty years down the road (although that's important), but in where they will be at the end of their critical first year—because this experience will give shape to what I pray will be a lifetime of joyful labors on behalf of Christ's people. So getting future pastors ready for day one at their first church is the burden of my work.

What follows is some help on how to approach the first year of pastoral ministry. If young ministers find it helpful, then I will be most grateful to God and deeply satisfied.

Acknowledgments

My FATHER, George Thomas Wingard Jr., taught me the fundamentals of pastoral care. More than anyone else, he prepared me for my first year of ministry. My uncle, John Calvin Wingard, has modeled faithful pastoral ministry during his long life, and even now, at age ninety-one, he continues to pastor and inspire.

I want to thank my congregations: Faith Presbyterian Church, Morganton, North Carolina; First Presbyterian Church North Shore, Ipswich, Massachusetts; Presbyterian Church of Cape Cod, West Barnstable, Massachusetts; Westminster Presbyterian Church, Huntsville, Alabama; and First Presbyterian Church, Yazoo City, Mississippi.

My elders encouraged me in the writing of this book, as they do in all my church and seminary labors. I am grateful to God for Bob Bailey, Billy Bridgforth, William Carroll, John Michael Pillow, and Jimmy Sullivan, a godly group of men who care deeply for God's church and for me.

Bill Barcley, Jack Davis, Ligon Duncan, T. David Gordon, Guy Richardson, David Strain, Miles Van Pelt, and Guy Waters provided much-needed feedback and encouragement.

My teaching assistant, Kyle Brent, and my personal assistant, Lindsey Austin, have worked hard for me (and with good cheer).

I am grateful to John Hughes for his consistently helpful feedback.

And Lynne, thank you for reading this over and over again. I love you!

"But as for you, continue in what you have learned and have firmly believed, knowing from whom you learned it and how from childhood you have been acquainted with the sacred writings, which are able to make you wise for salvation through faith in Christ Jesus. All Scripture is breathed out by God and profitable for teaching, for reproof, for correction, and for training in righteousness, that the man of God may be complete, equipped for every good work."

—2 TIMOTHY 3:14–17

Introduction

I AM SO thankful that you are preparing for Christian ministry. When men are called and prepared to be pastors, it is a tangible sign that the Lord loves his church. He gives us shepherds.

I don't know your story, but I sensed the call to gospel ministry when I was fourteen years old. Even on my worst days, I don't want to do anything else. After accepting a call to Faith Presbyterian Church in Morganton, North Carolina, I was ordained on August 18, 1985. My ordination date is more important to me than my birthday, and each year Lynne celebrates with a card, a gift, and a spectacular dinner.

The work of a pastor is diverse: leading worship, preaching, teaching, evangelism, missions, home and hospital visitation, counseling, calling on potential members, training leaders, fund-raising, and leading building campaigns. I wouldn't want to do any one of those tasks exclusively, but taken as a whole, pastoral ministry is deeply satisfying and the variety of work is continually refreshing.

Some of my enthusiasm for ministry is due to the temperament the Lord gave me. Even in the most difficult times, when I face intractable problems, I am usually happy. Struggles with grief and disappointment are part of my story, but I have enjoyed the life and work that God has given me. At one critical time, I thought briefly about abandoning my calling, but good friends stuck with me and pulled me through.

I love my calling, in part, because of the way I was prepared for it. My father was a pastor, and he included me in his work. He taught me how to care for God's people. Before and during seminary, I was assigned churches as a pastoral student. So when I began work in my first ordained position, there were no big surprises. I had experienced it all before: sermon preparation, visitation, counseling, living on a small salary, preparing a budget, working through cash shortfalls, attending session meetings, church conflict, and dealing with criticism and disaffected members. There were setbacks during my first year of ordained ministry—some of them heartbreaking—but I was expecting them.

Joys abounded there, too—far more than disappointments. The Lord gave me the most loving and caring first church. But I knew that "success" is transient and that no period of life or ministry is without difficulties. My evangelical heritage teaches me that where the kingdom advances, Satan unleashes his fury. But we don't need to look to Satan as the source of our trials. They are the norm in a fallen world, and they come from the hand of our loving heavenly Father, who disciplines us for our good. If I had been expecting a parade of transformed lives, the universal praise of a congregation, and one spiritual victory after another, disappointment would have overwhelmed me. But I knew better—not just intellectually, but experientially.

Perhaps you have not been so fortunate. You sit down at your first session meeting, and you're the moderator. No one has ever talked to you about a church budget. Seminary may have provided you with helpful homiletical instruction, but instead of preaching a handful of times a year, you now have forty-five to fifty sermons to prepare—and twice that number, if you have a Sunday-evening service. Your family struggles to live on your modest salary. One of your officers wants you to marry his daughter to an unbeliever, and your refusal will disrupt your relationship with the family and maybe divide the church. You're staring across your desk at a couple whose marriage is shattered by adultery—an experience for which no

classroom can adequately prepare you. Buried under an ava-
lanche of work that is new to you, you face circumstances to
which you have had no time to adjust. Without the encouragement of your seminary friends and the counsel of professors
at hand, you question your ministerial fitness. Add to this mix
your wife and children, who have been uprooted from friends
and maybe even family, and who now face their own set of
trials. Frustration, turmoil, and doubt are inevitable.

Have you misunderstood the Lord's calling? Realistic
preparation for ministry can go a long way toward allaying the
doubt and fear that arise during your first year. I pray that my
story and reflections will help and encourage you as you plan
your pathway to the pastorate.

In 1980, I graduated from college and accepted a position
as a student pastor at a tiny church (average attendance: ten).
On my first trip there, I arrived just as an ambulance pulled
into the driveway across the street. A man had just died of a
heart attack at the dinner table. My introduction to his elderly
parents, who were members of my new congregation, came
as EMTs worked to revive their son, and they were looking to
me for help. A short time later, I was counseling two families
traumatized by domestic violence, and meeting a father who
had just lost his teenage daughter in a tragic accident.

Even after many years, situations like these still send me to
the Lord in tears. Because I had a mentor to call upon and had
grown up in a pastor's home, I had some sense of what to do.
Otherwise, I don't know what I would have done. And it's the
not knowing that makes ministry frustrating—even miserable.

Your first year brings new relationships, many of them
completely unlike any you've known before. Think about
your present situation. You and your wife may be very popular. Until now, you have selected your friends carefully, are
esteemed by them, and share similar outlooks. You have kept

your distance from others, not wanting to invest yourself. This approach ends with your first church.

You don't select the members of your church. For the first time in your life, apart from your family, you're forced to live close to people you did not choose. Moreover, criticism of your work, some of it severe, comes at a time when you're unsure of yourself and your abilities. As time goes on, you learn to live with your shortcomings, but just out of the starting gate, even moderate criticism can be crushing.

The purpose of this little book is to help you navigate your first year of ministry. It is not a theology of ministry. Many fine books on that are available, and I can't improve on them. In "Readings in Preaching and Pastoral Theology" at the end of this book, I list books on preaching and pastoral care that have been my friends for years; I commend them to you.

This is not a comprehensive book on how to shepherd God's flock. You'll find such works in "Readings in Preaching and Pastoral Theology," too. My focus is on a few critical, nuts-and-bolts issues that will give you a good start. I seek to be suggestive, not prescriptive—sharing what I have found useful.

We will focus on four areas: preaching, pastoral care, administration, and caring for yourself and your family. Conspicuous by their absence are traditional categories like Christian education, evangelism, and community outreach. My reasoning is simple: young pastors try to do too much. Overwhelmed with new responsibilities, they also try to begin new programs. That is a mistake. Instead, we will look at ways that you can incorporate Christian education, evangelism, and community outreach into the routine work of preaching and pastoral care. My goal is to encourage you to focus on a few things, learning both to love them and to do them well.

If you read this book before you graduate from seminary, I want to outline some strategies for maximizing your ministerial preparation before ordination. If you're reading this during your early ministry, I want to suggest a way to prioritize your responsibilities. Not everything is critical to a good start. I want you to focus on the essentials.

Since my ordination, I have served five congregations. Two were near large seminaries, which gave me mentoring opportunities that have helped me identify and understand the skills that are needed by a young pastor, but that are often not obtained in seminary.

I have also worked for periods of time as a solo pastor—without staff or much in the way of financial resources. If this is where the Lord has placed you, then I understand if you're a bit intimidated or even frightened. I want to challenge you to take another look at your situation. Look clearly at its opportunities to lead and care for the flock, all the time trusting God for his provision. You occupy the single best training ground for a lifetime of fruitful ministry.

As you prepare for your first year, I want you to love the work of the pastor as much as I do.

"Whenever a young man comes forward, and tells us that he is called to the ministry, let us examine him rigidly, according to our excellent discipline and the requisitions of God's word. It is not enough that he tells us God has called him; let him show the evidences of his call."
—DANIEL A. PAYNE[1]

"So flee youthful passions and pursue righteousness, faith, love, and peace, along with those who call on the Lord from a pure heart. Have nothing to do with foolish, ignorant controversies; you know that they breed quarrels. And the Lord's servant must not be quarrelsome but kind to everyone, able to teach, patiently enduring evil, correcting his opponents with gentleness. God may perhaps grant them repentance leading to a knowledge of the truth, and they may come to their senses and escape from the snare of the devil, after being captured by him to do his will."
—2 TIMOTHY 2:22–26

"So I exhort the elders among you, as a fellow elder and a witness of the sufferings of Christ, as well as a partaker in the glory that is going to be revealed: shepherd the flock of God that is among you, exercising oversight, not under compulsion, but willingly, as God would have you; not for shameful gain, but eagerly; not domineering over those in your charge, but being examples to the flock. And when the chief Shepherd appears, you will receive the unfading crown of glory."
—1 PETER 5:1–4

1

Understanding Your Call to Ministry

OBJECTIVE: To consider carefully what it means for you to be called to gospel ministry.

BEFORE WE BEGIN, I'll touch first on the foundation—your call to ministry. Unless called by God, you must not enter the pastorate. Each sermon you preach, each act of pastoral care, and each prayer for your flock must be faithful to your calling.

Even if you are already ordained, I recommend that you read this chapter. Both veteran and new pastors need to consider the gravity of God's call. But when you are just beginning to sense that God is directing your steps toward pastoral ministry, careful thought about calling is especially critical. The cares of life and ministry can rob even the most devoted pastor of the urgency that once marked his ministry.

There's never a bad time to think about what it means to be called to ministry.

Since this book has the new pastor in mind, I'll begin with the critical question: "Am I called to pastoral ministry?" My aim is to make sure that you have thought carefully and prayerfully about the life and work of the pastor.

If you're uncertain, I want to help you discern whether

in fact you *are* called. To pursue pastoral ministry without a proper call will hurt you, your family, and the church of God—outcomes from which I want to protect you.

Consider the Office of the Minister

To understand your call to ministry, you must first think clearly about the office. What is the nature of the minister's office?

A good place to begin is with the scriptural titles given to ministers. Each one is a window into the soul of ministry.

As an *elder*, the minister serves as a father in the church, and his life is distinguished by maturity, wisdom, and godly character. As an *overseer*, he skillfully administers the affairs of the church. As a *steward of the mysteries of God*, he handles the Word and sacraments with reverent care. He is a *preacher*, a herald of the gospel, and an *ambassador*, earnestly pleading with sinners to be reconciled to God in Christ.[1]

The minister is also a *shepherd* (pastor) and a *teacher*.[2]

As a shepherd, you will feed, guide, and protect God's church. Your responsibilities will not be discharged from a remote and secure location. Instead, you will place yourself alongside God's people—living in their community, bearing their burdens, sharing their joys and sorrows—all the while interceding before the throne of grace for their welfare. You will take your cues from the Lord himself, the mighty God who tends his flock like a shepherd and gathers the lambs in his arms.[3]

You will be present with them to instruct, pray, counsel, admonish, and encourage. During your ministry, you may

1. Titus 1:5, 7; 1 Cor. 4:1; Rom. 10:14–15; 2 Cor. 5:20.
2. Eph. 4:11.
3. Isa. 40:11.

learn to use letters, podcasts, blog posts, and emails, but there is no substitute for being physically present with your people.

A minister is a shepherd, but he is a specific kind of shepherd: a *teaching* shepherd. God gathers, saves, sanctifies, and sustains his flock by his Word. Whether in pulpits, homes, hospitals, or jails, you will always be teaching.

Consider the Trials of the Minister

The literal shepherding of sheep is rewarding but arduous work. So, too, is shepherding God's church.

I love my work. I never wish that I were doing anything else; more satisfying work is unimaginable to me. My desire is that you would enjoy the work of the minister as much as I do, but you won't unless you are firmly persuaded of your calling.

Here's why: you will face trials, hardships, and spiritual enemies that will tempt you to run away. There is no escaping adversity. Unless you are firmly persuaded that God has summoned you to pastoral ministry, you will falter, grow weary, become discouraged, and fail.

John the Baptist was not a Christian minister, but the last of the Old Testament prophets—men who were called by God to proclaim his infallible Word. One Gospel writer describes him: "There was a man sent from God, whose name was John" (John 1:6). Had John not been convinced that he was called and sent by God, he would have crumbled under the privations of the wilderness. Or, fearful of the consequences, he would not have preached repentance to adulterous Herod and Herodias. And had he somehow, through strength of will, persevered in speaking the truth to them, he would have later succumbed to despair in the torments of Herod's prison.

John's suffering was uncommonly intense, far more so than yours and mine will ever be. Nevertheless, the sufferings that accompany your ministry will be real, and unless you are convinced that God has sent you to your congregation, your work will become unceasingly frustrating, leaving you bitter and burned out.

Consider the Internal and External Call of the Minister

God called John in an extraordinary manner, but he calls his new covenant ministers in a different way. How does God call his ministers?

Students of the Word have long observed that God's call is both internal and external. Internally, God is at work, renovating the life of the one he calls. Externally, the Lord is preparing the church to call and welcome his minister. The internal and external aspects of God's call are inseparable. Throughout the entire process of discernment, you want to examine your life and listen to your church.

Examine your life. Is there evidence of God's internal call? Look for:

- A clear understanding that you possess the scriptural qualifications of those set apart to minister God's Word;
- An awareness that the Holy Spirit has created within you a compulsion to perform the work of ministry; and
- The gifts and abilities necessary to fulfill your ministerial duties: an intellect capable of serious and sustained study, the ability to teach clearly, a love for God's people, and the conviction that gospel ministry must be your life's dominant work.

Listen to your church. What about the external call? As you examine your life, also listen to your church. Do the elders concur that you are, in fact, called to ministry? Are they willing to recommend that your presbytery make you a candidate for the ministry? Do your seminary professors see the intellectual gifting and godly comportment of a minister? Are churches providing you opportunities to preach, teach, and exercise other ministerial responsibilities? Are they affirming the spiritual value of your work? After the time of testing is complete, is there a congregation ready to call you as pastor? Your calling is complete only when presbytery approves the congregation's call.

Consider the Character and Skills of the Minister

Now let's think about the character traits and skills you must possess. Timothy and Titus were young ministers sent to serve in Ephesus and Crete. In Paul's two letters to Timothy and one to Titus, he establishes the divinely approved pattern for the minister and his work.

Two specific lists of ministerial qualifications are found in these letters, in 1 Timothy 3:1–7 and Titus 1:5–9. As you read these passages, keep in mind both the internal and the external aspects of your call:

> The saying is trustworthy: If anyone aspires to the office of overseer, he desires a noble task. Therefore an overseer must be above reproach, the husband of one wife, sober-minded, self-controlled, respectable, hospitable, able to teach, not a drunkard, not violent but gentle, not quarrelsome, not a lover of money. He must manage his own household well, with all dignity keeping his children submissive, for if someone does not know how to manage his own household, how will he care for God's church? He must not be a recent convert, or he may become puffed up with conceit

and fall into the condemnation of the devil. Moreover, he must be well thought of by outsiders, so that he may not fall into disgrace, into a snare of the devil. (1 Tim. 3:1–7)

This is why I left you in Crete, so that you might put what remained into order, and appoint elders in every town as I directed you—if anyone is above reproach, the husband of one wife, and his children are believers and not open to the charge of debauchery or insubordination. For an overseer, as God's steward, must be above reproach. He must not be arrogant or quick-tempered or a drunkard or violent or greedy for gain, but hospitable, a lover of good, self-controlled, upright, holy, and disciplined. He must hold firm to the trustworthy word as taught, so that he may be able to give instruction in sound doctrine and also to rebuke those who contradict it. (Titus 1:5–9)

Let's examine these qualifications.

Conversion

The minister "must not be a recent convert." But he must be a convert! An unconverted minister is worse than useless; he threatens the existence of a congregation. His prayerlessness and lack of concern for the things of God and for the spiritual welfare of the people of God are an abomination to the Lord.

Are you converted? Are you persuaded that you are lost and condemned, apart from the mercy of God in Jesus Christ? Have you forsaken all hope of salvation by your own merits? Are you trusting alone for salvation in the righteousness and blood of the Savior? Are you conscious, day by day, of your need for divine forgiveness and the renewing power of the Holy Spirit?

When you were admitted to the communicant membership of God's church, your church's elders examined you. They sought clear evidence of your faith and repentance. Now, at every step in the ordination process—from your first meeting with presbytery to the calling of a local congregation—you will be asked to supply a credible testimony of faith and repentance.

Aspiration

"If anyone aspires to the office of overseer, he desires a noble task."[4] Do you have an inward compulsion to shepherd God's church? Does ministry shape your heart? Can you echo Paul's testimony: "Woe to me if I do not preach the gospel!"[5]

Someone has said that a man should not be in ministry if he can do any other work. That doesn't mean that you are so wretchedly unskilled that you couldn't support yourself in another occupation. If that were true, we would be a sorry lot. What it *does* mean is that because God's calling has obligated you to ministry, you can never be content in a vocation that precludes gospel work.

When I am interviewing associates, I am always looking for men who love God and the work of ministry. The reason is simple: when God calls a man to gospel work, he creates within him a love for ministry. That passion is evident to the one who is called; it must also be evident to the church that calls him.

---

4. In the Presbyterian tradition, a distinction is made between ruling elders (those who rule in God's church) and teaching elders (those who rule and teach). The minister serves in the latter role. That distinction, while important, is not the burden of this chapter.

5. 1 Cor. 9:16.

Skilled Leadership

The minister "must manage his own household well, with all dignity keeping his children submissive, for if someone does not know how to manage his own household, how will he care for God's church?" Of course, this requirement includes raising children in the fear and admonition of the Lord—but also much more. Many ancient homes included business operations, complex financial arrangements, and the supervision of personnel (household servants). If a man managed these affairs poorly, he would also be a poor manager of God's church.

Every job you undertake, every course of study you pursue, and every child you raise reflects upon your fitness to lead. Throughout your preparations for ministry, you build a record. Are you meeting these challenges competently? Do your church and your presbytery recognize your competence?

It may be helpful to reflect upon one area of life that many ministerial candidates find especially challenging: supporting a family financially while in seminary. Navigating this stressful time and leaving seminary without enslaving debt is one indication that you can manage family and church well.

Keep in mind that the church that calls you has every right to expect you to have what the business world identifies as "marketable skills." That is, you must be able to gather, nourish, and fortify God's church, and raise money to meet a budget. Only a careless church would call a man without those skills.

Character

Your character counts. The minister must be "above reproach," which means that no credible charge of false doctrine or scandalous behavior may be brought against him.

Therefore, as you read these passages, ask yourself: Do these virtues describe me? Am I sober-minded, self-controlled, and not arrogant, quick-tempered, a drunkard, violent, or greedy for gain? Am I hospitable and a lover of good? Although a sinner, am I, by the grace of God, upright, holy, and disciplined?

Space does not permit sustained reflection on these virtues. Therefore, take the time to consult solid commentaries on the letters to Timothy and Titus.[6]

Relationships

One aspect of character needs particular attention: strong and healthy relationships. "The husband of one wife" means that the minister's uncompromising sexual fidelity to his wife is a given. Both adultery and the indulgence of pornographic material disqualify a man from ministry. No man engaged in either can expect God's blessing.

The minister's life is also marked by sobriety and self-control, both in his private and in his public life. Conflict is an inevitable part of life and ministry, and the minister must maintain his poise in controversy. He refuses to quarrel; he abhors angry words.

A minister's relationships must be healthy, both inside and outside the church. A Christian minister is a public figure. He is known in his community. He will interact with people in its activities, shopping centers, schools, and athletic events. Many of those with whom he comes into contact will not be Christians. He must cultivate good relationships with them. He lives in such a way as to "be well thought of by outsiders."

6. I recommend Patrick Fairbairn, *A Commentary on 1 and 2 Timothy* (Grand Rapids: Zondervan, 1956), and George W. Knight, *The Pastoral Epistles: A Commentary on the Greek Text*, NIGTC (Grand Rapids: Eerdmans, 1992).

Before you read further, stop and reflect: inside and outside the church, are you known as a man of sexual integrity, gracious speech, and goodwill?

Teaching Competency

The minister must be "able to teach" and "hold firm to the trustworthy word as taught, so that he may be able to give instruction in sound doctrine and also to rebuke those who contradict it." Throughout your time of preparation, you will be cultivating your teaching gifts. Do the congregations you teach (and the ministers and professors who hear you preach) affirm your gifts? One of the clearest indications that you have teaching gifts is the desire of people to hear you teach.

Conclusion

Don't expect a heavenly voice or vision to confirm your call to ministry. That is not how God summons his ministers.

Do expect a considerable amount of time to pass as you evaluate your life, cultivate your skills, and look to the church for confirmation of God's gifting of you for ministry.

Be patient with yourself. Study the Bible carefully. Receive the counsel of God's people. Keep yourself before the Lord in prayer, always seeking the gifts and graces you will need to serve his church and crucifying those sins that would mar your life and ministry.

"They that are called to labor in the ministry of the Word, are to preach sound doctrine, diligently, in season and out of season; plainly, not in the enticing words of man's wisdom, but in demonstration of the Spirit, and of power; faithfully, making known the whole counsel of God; wisely, applying themselves to the necessities and capacities of the hearers; zealously, with fervent love to God and the souls of his people; sincerely, aiming at his glory, and their conversion, edification, and salvation."

—WESTMINSTER LARGER CATECHISM 159

"Dr. Wilbur Chapman has this to say of the handicaps which befall the minister: 'When trials are many, when burdens are heavy, when tears are blinding, when the heart is almost broken, then, as a rule, ministers come to an experience when effective preaching is possible.'"

—WILLIAM CHILDS ROBINSON[2]

"Have nothing to do with irreverent, silly myths. Rather train yourself for godliness; for while bodily training is of some value, godliness is of value in every way, as it holds promise for the present life and also for the life to come."

—1 TIMOTHY 4:7–8

"Do your best to present yourself to God as one approved, a worker who has no need to be ashamed, rightly handling the word of truth."

—2 TIMOTHY 2:15

2

Preparing for Pulpit Ministry

OBJECTIVE: To order your life and studies to prepare you to preach. Seize every opportunity to cultivate your preaching gifts.

YOU MUST BE able to preach—not just stand up and talk, but preach and preach well. You are a herald of God and an ambassador of Christ. A man who can't preach should not be a pastor, for preaching is the pastor's preeminent work. My goal is for you to arrive at your first church ready to preach.

In the next chapter, we'll look at sermon preparation. But for now, let's think about the preparation for pulpit ministry that must take place before your ordination. I urge you to pay attention to your education, mentors, preaching opportunities, and sermon feedback.

Obtain the Right Education

If you are a high school student selecting a college, here's my advice: attend a liberal arts college that introduces you to as many fields as possible during your four years. My collegiate studies in political science, history, literature, and philosophy became lifelong interests that have deepened my understanding of God's complex world—the world in which the members of my congregations live and work. My education checked the temptation to treat my era and nation as either the zenith of civilization or the nadir of human depravity.

A well-rounded liberal arts education emphasizes the composition skills necessary for effective communication, both written and oral. Don't avoid demanding teachers who have rigorous standards. Instead, seek them out. Time is too valuable to waste on substandard professors and easy classes. You will leave poor classes no more ready for ministry than when you entered. Professors who push you hard are God's gift. They prepare you for a lifetime of serious study and exposition.

I am satisfied with my undergraduate training. Still, there are some things I would change if I could do it over. The two and a half years of French would give way to biblical Greek and Hebrew, the foundation of studies in pastoral ministry. For many, including me, learning the biblical languages is the most difficult aspect of seminary training. Greek was not an option in my primary and secondary education, so college would have been the ideal place to learn it.

Taking biblical languages at the same time as other seminary courses is akin to simultaneously laying a foundation and erecting the superstructure—a method any contractor would find preposterous. I urge you, if possible, to begin your biblical language studies before entering seminary.

A final word, directed to the lazy, distracted, and half-hearted: students who won't take their collegiate studies seriously won't take seminary studies seriously, either. More importantly, they prove themselves unfit to serve as ministers, men set apart for the lifelong study of God's Word. Please don't let that be you!

Develop a Seminary Strategy

If you're thinking about seminary, explore schools whose faculties are distinguished by sound theology, holiness of life, and pastoral experience. Professors with pastoral experience will help you connect the dots between what you learn in the classroom and its application to the life of the church. I'll say more about selecting a seminary later.

When you arrive at seminary, quickly establish routines and habits that will maximize your time of preparation. Pay attention especially to five strategies.

1. Find a church home quickly. Sanctification of the Lord's Day, sitting under God's Word preached, receiving the Lord's Supper, and caring for and being cared for by God's people are indispensable to *your* spiritual well-being and (if married) *your family's*. Don't prolong your search.

Your adjustment may be tough. Don't be discouraged. It's part of your preparation for ministry. All pastors work with people who struggle to fit into new church homes. A few years from now, you will, too. Therefore, right now, your and your family's struggles to fit in are equipping you for ministry. Through such difficulties, God is making you a sympathetic shepherd.

2. Don't pit your studies against your devotional life. During my first year at Princeton, I stumbled upon a copy of B. B. Warfield's *The Religious Life of Theological Students* and received perhaps the most helpful counsel of my seminary career: *make your turning to the books a turning to God.*[1] Before you open a text, ask the Lord to bless your reading with an increased knowledge of his character and of your need

1. Benjamin Breckinridge Warfield, "The Religious Life of Theological Students," *The Master's Seminary Journal* 6, 2 (Fall 1995): 182, https://www.tms.edu/m/tmsj6g.pdf (accessed September 18, 2017).

of grace. Read to obtain a deeper understanding of his Word and of the world. Fill your time in the books with prayers of adoration, thanksgiving, confession, repentance, and renewal. If you do, you'll establish enduring study habits to the glory of God.

3. Guard your study time. Most of us get only one shot at seminary; misuse the time, and you will finish your studies inadequately prepared. Even if it were possible to learn later what you miss now, the opportunity costs are steep. For years, you will labor without the benefit of what could have been yours from the start.

On campus and in church, you will be asked to serve in many ways. Before you say yes, make sure that your studies are squared away. Take to heart the old adage: "Do what you have to do, then do what you want to do."

Don't succumb to the temptation of thinking of your studies as competition to serving the Lord. Right now, your studies *are* your primary field of service. Should you serve in other ways? Most definitely, but not before you are sure you can meet your academic requirements.

4. Watch your spending. Most of the time, family conflict about money has its roots not in scarcity, but in negligence. Many students and their spouses don't think carefully about their finances. The consequences can be dire: strained relationships, overwork, and, sometimes, withdrawal from seminary and the abandoning of plans for ministry. Don't let that be your story. Spend less than you earn; get and stay on a budget; put on paper where your money will go. If you don't know how to do that, ask for help—and the sooner, the better.

It breaks my heart to hear stories of men who prepare for ministry, but then must turn down a pastoral call because their debt makes it impossible. Learn the fundamentals of financial management now, and reap its rewards for a lifetime.

5. Eliminate distractions when you're studying, at home, and with the Lord. When you set aside time to study, be fully engaged. Turn off email and all notifications; silence your cell phone; refuse to surf the Web.

When you return home, give your wife and children your full attention; put your phone, books, and computer away.

During your personal devotions, be fully engaged with the Lord and his Word.

When you eliminate distractions and concentrate on the task before you, you'll be surprised at how much you accomplish and grow in your work and relationships.

Seminary has its share of opportunities and trials. The lessons learned here will go with you to your first church. Resolve to make these habits your own, and they, too, will follow you throughout your ministry.

Find a Good Mentor

While at college and seminary, find a church where the pastor sets high standards of pulpit ministry and pastoral care, and who is willing to work with you. Under his tutelage, you will learn what the pastorate is all about. He will also help you understand how academic life prepares you to become a minister of the Word.

Sitting each week under good preaching and teaching is invaluable. Week by week you arrive at church desiring to be nourished in the Word, just like everyone else. But you will receive more than instruction. Each week your pastor will model how to deliver a sermon. So think carefully about whose preaching you sit under. Is this a man whose personal example will make you a more effective preacher of God's Word?

Campus ministers who serve local congregations are also potential role models. They frequently set a high standard of compassionate pastoral care and teaching. Is there one on your campus who is willing to work with you as you prepare for ministry?

I cannot overemphasize the importance of a good mentor. As a professor of pastoral theology, I want to give my students the best possible instruction in pastoral care. Class readings are selected carefully, and the lectures are designed to equip students to skillfully serve their first flock. That said, I cannot give my students what my dad gave me—the daily example of faithfully caring for God's church. He was my dad *and* my mentor. Nor can I give my students the hands-on training of a skilled mentor-pastor. My job is to supplement the work of mentors.

So watch your mentors. Ask questions. Listen attentively. Study their lives.

Watch How Good Preachers Craft and Deliver Their Sermons

In 1979, I attended Urbana and marveled as John Stott opened up the first few chapters of Romans. His expository style was worthy of imitation. In fact, I resolved to preach like him (or at least try!), and he has been a role model ever since.

Read Voraciously

Martyn Lloyd-Jones's sermons on Ephesians convinced me that expository preaching through books of the Bible is the single most effective way of proclaiming the whole counsel of God—and it has been my method for thirty-seven years. William Childs Robinson's splendid *The Word of the Cross* showed me how to keep my preaching focused on Christ and his work.

Study the lives of men who were greatly used by God. At the start of my work as a student pastor, a friend of my dad gave me Arnold Dallimore's two-volume biography of George

Whitefield. Thus began a habit of reading serious biographies and autobiographies of ministers and missionaries. I am always reading them, one right after another. In such books, you'll find that the struggles you face in ministry are nothing new. Others have faced them and persevered. So will you. You'll learn from their successes and failures. You'll take your place among the company of faithful pastors who have served God's flock from generation to generation.

Seek Opportunities to Preach

Soon after I graduated from college in 1980, I crammed all my possessions into a 1970 Chevrolet Impala and set out for my first churches. As student pastor, I served a field of four widely scattered rural congregations in Middle Tennessee. That year I preached some ninety times. While in seminary, I pastored two more rural congregations, and preached two or three times each Lord's Day. Boots-on-the-ground experience made me confident that the Lord would supply whatever I needed to minister the gospel.

Many factors go into deciding where you should attend seminary. One of them should be the opportunity to preach often. A strength of the seminary in which I serve is that we get men out on the preaching circuit—churches that are without pastors and are looking to our seminary to fill their pulpits. If our students seize the opportunities, accept feedback, and labor in faith, they will graduate and show up at their first church prepared to preach. Congregations will benefit from their youth *and* their experience!

Preaching labs and occasional preaching during internships are fine, but they are no substitute for preaching thirty or more times a year while in seminary. Find vacant pulpits and offer your services. Go to jails and nursing homes. Get on schools' chapel schedules. Skip the young adults' Sunday school class and volunteer to teach children. Whatever you must do to make it happen, preach. And when pulpits aren't available, teach.

Cultivate Your Speaking Gifts

Get as much preaching experience as you can before and during seminary.

Be alert for opportunities outside the church. Join a debate team or Toastmasters—get a feel for what it's like to address groups. Solicit group feedback. To show up at your first church with only sporadic public speaking experience is unwise. Why not bring as much experience as possible to your first pastorate?[2]

During your final year, you will send out résumés as you search for a call to your first church. The thought of becoming a solo pastor, with its myriad of responsibilities, intimidates you. So why not join a church staff and get more experience under your belt?

That may be a good option for you. Serving on a larger church's staff provides valuable opportunities to learn about church administration and staff management, to enjoy the camaraderie and mentoring of senior staff, and to prepare for future service. These advantages are significant, especially if you have had little leadership experience.

Still, I advise you not to quickly dismiss the solo pastorate.

---

2. The strict licensure requirements of my own denomination make it difficult for young men to preach before seminary. I don't for a moment wish to reduce licensure or ordination standards. However, I'm convinced that it's not good for a solo pastor to begin his work without regular preaching experience. One way to maintain high licensure and ordination standards while cultivating preaching gifts early in a man's candidacy for ministry would be to grant mentor pastors permission to approve specific sermons of ministerial candidates. Standards of orthodoxy would be maintained while providing the candidates with precious pulpit experience.

The advantages of beginning in a small church are real. You will preach one or more times a week. Seminary graduates often join the staff of a larger church only to discover that they seldom preach. And when they move on to a solo or senior pastor position, they are only a little bit better prepared to preach than when they left seminary. Whatever its challenges, a solo pastorate offers abundant time in the pulpit. Take this advantage seriously.

Another advantage of a solo pastorate is that you will obtain comprehensive pastoral experience in ministering to the entire congregation. Frequently, assuming a staff position will lock you into a situation that narrows the range of your ministry as you serve predominantly youth or seniors or some other group within the church.

I have been a senior pastor for most of my ministry. My desire has been to hire associate pastors who are interested in becoming senior pastors. Here's my deal with them: if they provide competent leadership in a narrow area of ministry, then I will provide them with extensive experience in each major area of pastoral ministry.

For example, my associates may lead youth and family ministry that includes the youth and family programs. The associate's retention will depend on his successful leadership in that area. I give him wide latitude to organize and manage his sphere as he sees fit. As the new associate demonstrates competency here, I begin to turn over to him other areas of responsibility: preaching at the Sunday evening service, and serving on various committees to obtain experience in finances, capital campaigns, and mercy ministries. From the start, he will make hospital and pastoral visits with me until he is comfortable making the visits himself.

After a year of attending session meetings, he is provided with the opportunity to draft agendas and moderate meetings.

If a man has served with me three or more years, I want him to be able to tell a pulpit committee that he has at one time or another discharged *all* the duties of a senior pastor, and that he has preached forty or more sermons a year (evening services and the Sunday morning services when I am away).

I ask my associates to let me know when they are ready to seek a senior pastoral (or other) position. From day one, they have my pledge to do all I can to help them. I also want my elders and congregations on board with the goal of training young men for senior pastoral positions.

Solicit Sermon Feedback

Take sermon feedback from every quarter and prize it like gold. Ask your mentor pastor and professors for their evaluations of your sermons. Perhaps an older minister will agree to listen to occasional recordings and provide you with constructive criticism.

Dr. Gwyn Walters, a retired professor of preaching at Gordon-Conwell Theological Seminary, attended my church. While I was visiting him at home, he offered to help me with my preaching. Fighting cancer and unable to preach on the Lord's Day, he found the strength to meet with me three hours a week for eighteen months. His earnest concern and counsel made all the difference in the world to me, both as a man and as a preacher.

One of my associate pastors asked a retired minister who lived in another state to evaluate some of his sermons online. They spoke by phone regularly.

At one church, I distributed index cards to five people at a time, each with three questions: What was the main point of the sermon? What did you find helpful about the sermon? What was unhelpful?

Honest feedback is sobering. After hearing me preach a sermon on predestination, a young lady wrote that she was relieved that she didn't have to worry about evangelism. That was not my point at all! But I need to know what people hear—not what I *think* they hear.

Early in my ministry at a new church, I preached on Ephesians 2:8–10. One dear lady complained that the sermon reeked of Calvinism (she got the part about faith as God's gift, and chose to raise her objection to me and not Paul). A man who heard the same message was almost giddy; he appreciated the evangelistic tenor of the message. He zeroed in on my exhortations to receive and rest upon Christ alone for salvation. He went so far as to say that he liked the sermon because it had no doctrine! What an eye-opener that was: two people heard the same message; one deemed me a dour Calvinist, the other an evangelist without doctrine. What I learned from these two exchanges was important: the congregation, as a whole, was theologically diverse and had had little instruction in its own confessional standards, and a theological foundation needed to be laid.

Church members want to encourage you, especially when you're young and learning the ropes. Don't disappoint them; make them your partners. When they say that they find your sermon helpful, ask them why. "What about the sermon encouraged you?" Tell them that you want to grow as a preacher and that their feedback is vital. Then listen carefully.

Feedback also corrects bad habits. At one time, I punctuated my sentences liberally with "uh." You know what I'm talking about, uh, like when a minister says, uh, that we should walk in the paths of righteousness, uh. On her feedback card, one woman noted that I muttered the meaningless monosyllable forty-eight times during the course of the sermon— a terribly irritating distraction. I asked her to keep counting each week, which she did until I worked my way down to three "uhs." Later, a New Englander complained that I incorrectly pronounced "can't" as "cain't." "That may play in the South, but not in Massachusetts," she warned.

Why needlessly mar the proclamation of God's Word by lack of clarity or by a bad habit? Feedback helps. Profusely thank those people who care enough about your work to speak honestly. Don't be defensive. In each church I have served, most of the members have rooted for me to be a good preacher. Why shouldn't I accept their criticisms and encouragements as gifts from my heavenly Father, who loves both them and me?

Many church sessions conduct annual performance reviews of their pastors. I am skeptical of their value. As someone has said, annual feedback is not *regular* feedback. If substantial problems exist, negative criticism submitted all at once can be overwhelming. So obtain routine feedback from your elders, both privately and at elders' meetings. But keep this in mind: your elders will be among the most biblically and theologically literate people in your congregation. You must also solicit the feedback of others who are at various stages of their Christian lives and maturity.

Before your ordination, serious study, seasoned mentors, regular preaching, and helpful feedback are treasures to be sought and cherished.

"Bring everything you have and are to your ministry—your best crafts-manship, your most concentrated study, your truest technique, your uttermost of self-consecration, your toil and sweat of brain and heart—bring it all without reserve. But when you have brought it, something else remains: Stand back, and see the salvation of God."
—JAMES S. STEWART[3]

"But a man preacheth that sermon only well unto others which preacheth itself in his own soul. And he that doth not feed on and thrive in the digestion of the food which he provides for others will scarce make it savoury unto them; yea, he knows not but the food he hath pro-vided may be poison, unless he have really tasted of it himself. If the word do not dwell with power in us, it will not pass with power from us."
—JOHN OWEN[4]

"How then will they call on him in whom they have not believed? And how are they to believe in him of whom they have never heard? And how are they to hear without someone preaching? And how are they to preach unless they are sent? As it is written, 'How beautiful are the feet of those who preach the good news!'"
—ROMANS 10:14–15

"For what we proclaim is not ourselves, but Jesus Christ as Lord, with ourselves as your servants for Jesus' sake."
—2 CORINTHIANS 4:5

"[Christ] we proclaim, warning everyone and teaching everyone with all wisdom, that we may present everyone mature in Christ. For this I toil, struggling with all his energy that he powerfully works within me."
—COLOSSIANS 1:28–29

"Preach the word; be ready in season and out of season; reprove, rebuke, and exhort, with complete patience and teaching."
—2 TIMOTHY 4:2

3

Preparing and Delivering a Sermon

OBJECTIVE: To take thoughtful and organized steps to prepare and deliver your sermons.

FAITHFUL MINISTERS MAKE preaching a priority. They know that sermon preparation is labor-intensive and that time is a fixed commodity. Every preacher has exactly 168 hours to get ready to preach. Managing that precious time is indispensable to fruitful pulpit ministry.

What does your use of time say about the importance you attach to sermon preparation and delivery?

A reliable indicator of your commitment is your calendar and work diary. If someone were to look at them, would that person immediately sense that you plan for concentrated, exclusive, and uninterrupted preparation during the week? You devote your invaluable time to the things that matter most. Is preaching one of them?

If the time you give to sermon preparation is sporadic and unpredictable, then it is possible that you fail to value it as God does. The Westminster Larger Catechism captures God's estimation of preaching when it declares: "The Spirit of God maketh the reading, *but especially the preaching of the Word*, an effectual means of enlightening, convincing, and humbling sinners; of driving them out of themselves, and drawing them unto Christ; of conforming them to his image, and subduing them to his will; of strengthening them against temptations and corruptions; of building them up in grace, and establishing their hearts in holiness and comfort through faith unto salvation."[1] When the Word of God is preached, the Spirit of God is doing his enlightening, convincing, humbling, driving, drawing, conforming, subduing, strengthening, and establishing work. The godly preacher wants to give his best to this.

It's one thing to understand the value of preaching; it's quite another to develop habits that reflect its value. Here are some steps you can take to use your time efficiently.

Plan Your Month, Week, and Day

If you don't schedule time for sermon preparation, you will always be a slave to the vicissitudes of pastoral life. Counseling, meetings, visits, and crises will dominate your days and leave little room for serious study. Therefore, make your calendar your ally. Plan for prep time.

About my calendar: I use a combination analog and digital system to stay on track. During the last week of each quarter and month, I look ahead on my digital calendar to the coming quarter and month and then transfer major meetings and deadlines to my planner. Unless I have already done so, I create tasks for each event and insert them at their proper deadline. Every Friday, I put on my calendar all events for the coming week, and tasks are reviewed and new tasks created. Each night of the week, I check my calendar for the next day and make necessary changes. This may seem laborious, but keep in mind these advantages:

1. Westminster Larger Catechism 155.

- Nothing is left to memory, which I never trust.
- Distractions are reduced. For example, if, while I am reading, it pops into my mind that I need to make a phone call, I quickly put it on my task list and return to reading. To stop and make the phone call would break my concentration. To trust myself to remember to make that call later would be foolish.
- Writing may seem like an extra chore, but it prevents me from rapidly scanning my digital calendar and missing something important. Also, while I write, I think and pray about my obligations and how best to fulfill them. Writing slows down my work pace, but in a healthy way.
- I check my planner each morning and late afternoon or evening, and keep it open throughout the day.

Now, what does all this have to do with study? Everything! The time I will study goes on the calendar. I don't hope to study if time permits; I have a *plan* to study. Disorganization exacts a price in every area of life, including study, and long hours of study are crucial to a successful pulpit ministry.

No one routine fits all. We all approach our work with a varying set of traits—intellectual, physical, and imaginative. Still, it's helpful to learn how others tackle sermon preparation. Evaluate ideas about how to optimize your prep time, and accept, reject, or modify them. Find what suits you and get to work. But if you fail to plan, life will crowd out your precious study time.

Know the Time of Day When You Work Most Efficiently

I am an early riser, and the morning is my most productive and creative time of day—so I always try to reserve that time for study. Phone calls, emails, visits, and appointments come later. The trick here is not to turn yourself into an early riser, but to make sure that *your* best part of each day is reserved for the task of preparing your sermon.

Begin Working on Your Sermon Early in the Week

On Mondays, I begin to outline the sermon and write my manuscript. Although I don't advise preaching from a manuscript,[2] I do find it beneficial to write one sermon each week. Disciplined writing promotes clarity of thinking, precision of speech, and orderliness of presentation. If I am preaching twice on the Lord's Day, my second sermon is an abbreviated manuscript that contains an outline and content summary. That way I can return to the sermon later, know what I said, and preach the sermon again.

The initial outline will be revised throughout the week. Developing an outline forces you to think about how you will actually preach the passage. Make the outline simple, clear, and memorable. Your main points and subpoints are stepping stones that help people traverse the text. If you can't recite your outline from memory, it's too long. Later, if you think it necessary, write a more extended outline to take into the pulpit— things you don't want to forget. But this developing outline contains the points and subpoints that you want to impress upon the minds and hearts of your listeners. Refine it as the week moves along, but get started early.

Very early in the week, my manuscript begins to take shape. Thoughts and ideas go on paper, and a sermon starts to form.

2. For a thorough discussion on the strengths and weaknesses of preaching from a manuscript, see John A. Broadus, *On the Preparation and Delivery of Sermons* (Vestavia Hills, AL: Solid Ground Christian Books, 2005), 439–50.

In your manuscript, use spoken English. Write like you speak. Your sermon is not for publication, but for proclamation.

At first, I don't consult commentaries. Instead, I think and write first, and only later do some research. After all, it's not the first time I've read the text. In my daily Bible readings and seminary studies, I've already spent time with the passage. So I begin with what's primary—crafting in the presence of God what I will preach to his people. The sermon begins to take shape before other resources are consulted.

Some young preachers spend hours during the week translating the passage, consulting commentaries, and listening to other preachers' sermons. Only toward the end of the week do they begin writing. The hard labor is commendable, but the order is mistaken. It leaves sermon composition to the very last moment. What is presented to the congregation is hurriedly conceived and may lack clarity, persuasion, and depth. Commentaries and lexical aids come later for me, as I develop, refine, and sharpen points.

Use Commentaries Judiciously

Depending on how you use them, commentaries can be friends or foes. They are your enemies if you use them as a crutch. Preaching through a passage verse by verse and sharing what you've read in commentaries turn a sermon into a research paper (and a poor one at that). You deprive the congregation of what it needs most—your struggling with the text in the Lord's presence, in order to bring them his life-giving Word of grace.

Commentaries may be a distraction when the majority of your time is spent reading them and taking notes, while forfeiting the hours you need to think, pray, reflect, compose, and write your way clear.

But commentaries can be your most cherished friends if you use them to clarify the meaning of difficult passages, to identify suggestive ways of putting a text into its larger literary and canonical context, and to provide a summary of a passage's history of interpretation. Make sure that at least one of your commentaries is a technical commentary that works from the original Greek or Hebrew text.

Once you determine the meaning of the passage, preach it. In your sermon, don't sift through various interpretive options. You are an ambassador, not a professor. As Christ's ambassador, you proclaim the authoritative Word of our King! No ambassador says, "Here is one way of looking at my president's words, and here is another, and here is yet another." Rather, firmly grasping the content of the president's message, he delivers it. Similarly you, with authority and firmness of conviction, must proclaim God's Word!

In the course of a sermon series, I consult several commentaries. Some of them I read from cover to cover. Others I consult only when I need help understanding a difficult passage. Find the right balance. But after your study is done, what counts is the text. Explain, illustrate, and apply it, so that your flock will be well nourished in the Word. A pastor who loves his people will always feed his flock faithfully.

Don't Forget Systematic Theology

We approach every text as trained theologians, and we do not want our theological studies to lapse after graduation. Consider making one good book of systematic theology a companion as you prepare a sermon series. For example, as I write this chapter, I am preaching through Exodus. As I study, I consult the Scripture index of Herman Bavinck's four-volume systematic theology and read how these texts have shaped his understanding of God's character and work. When preaching on Exodus 9:16—God's word to Pharaoh, "But for this purpose I have raised you up, to show you my power, so that my name may be proclaimed in all the earth"—I found it most helpful to review Bavinck's thoughts on election, reprobation, and even the lapsarian controversy.

Systematic theology is invaluable. Its best writers help me to define clearly, concisely, and memorably theological terms like *Trinity, sin, guilt, incarnation, regeneration, justification, sanctification,* and a host of other words that are precious to every believer. Contemporary heresies that disrupt the church originate in the errors of previous generations, and systematic theology helps me identify and repudiate falsehood and defend the truth that God's church confesses and adores. Take your studies of systematic theology seriously, and you will find yourself a more knowledgeable ambassador of Christ, able to articulate the gospel message accurately and with compelling clarity.

Learn from Other Ministers' Sermons

Learn how other ministers expound the text, use illustrations, make applications, and appeal to conscience. But be careful. First, don't preach other men's sermons! That's theft and it's wrong. Besides, your congregation needs *you*—your gifts, your knowledge of their lives, and your pastoral wisdom.

I advise against listening to sermons as a routine method of preparing to preach on the Lord's Day. Listening to them is time-consuming. Relying on them instead of your own strenuous efforts may prove to be hard to resist. When I listen to other preachers, it is not part of my weekly sermon prep. Be the preacher that God has made you. Learn from other men, but never imitate them slavishly. God has sent you to *your* congregation, with *your* gifts and abilities, not someone else.

Listen to sermons during the time that you devote to study that is in addition to your sermon preparation. Make it a part of your continuing education and food for your soul.

Know Your Congregation

The annual Thanksgiving service was special in one of my congregations. Members stood up and recounted the Lord's blessings.

One year a young man took a seat in a different row from the rest of his family, which was highly unusual for him. During the time of sharing, he stood and pointed to his seat. It was where he had sat for worship a few years earlier, when the Lord spiritually awakened him during the sermon and brought him to faith in Christ.

The sermon I preached that Lord's Day was not exclusively evangelistic. But in every worship service I endeavor to keep before the congregation cardinal gospel truths: God is holy; we are sinful; there is a Savior available for us, able and willing to save; and by resting in him alone for salvation we can know that our sins are forgiven and we are reconciled to God. So I think about people like that young man when I preach. Is my sermon evangelical? Does it offer Christ as the one perfect sacrifice that reconciles poor sinners to God? Have I appealed to the listener's conscience, seeking to persuade him to be right with God through Jesus Christ? Am I earnestly pursuing his sanctification?

Think about your congregation. A variety of people assemble before you every Lord's Day: the unbeliever, the new Christian needing instruction, the tested saint who struggles to persevere for one more day, the self-righteous who must be humbled, the distraught craving hope, the backslider clinging to sin, the tempted seeking strength, and the grieving longing for comfort. As you prepare your sermon, think of these people and how to speak to them biblically, convincingly, and winsomely.[3]

Your congregation is a diverse group: the godly elder, the overwhelmed mother, the uninterested teenager, the skeptical college student, the angry father, the young woman pregnant out of wedlock, and the businessman on the brink of financial failure. Will they find conviction, comfort, hope, and assurance through the message you proclaim? Will they leave the place of worship convinced that God is for them in Christ Jesus? Will they have reason to be persuaded by what you preach that God is both their trustworthy Sovereign and their loving heavenly Father?

Sermons are the work of a shepherd, and every shepherd must pursue the appropriate combination of courage and humility, boldness and tact, firmness and gentleness, holy anger and sympathetic understanding.

Review Your Sermon Again and Again

My manuscript is ordinarily finished by midweek. On Saturday, I read through my sermon or extended outline *aloud* at least six times. The purpose is not to memorize the sermon, but to ensure that its contents are firmly fixed in my mind. As I read, I'm thinking about my words. Are they biblical? Are they clear?

As I review, I think about the people who will sit before me. Will the preached Word build them up in Christ? I pray for God's blessing on the sermon's various points. Some lines are crossed out; others are revised. Notes are added as new ideas come to mind.

---

3. To help you think about the various kinds of people in your congregation, I recommend William Perkins, *The Art of Prophesying* (Carlisle, PA: Banner of Truth, 1996), 54–63, and Charles Bridges, *The Christian Ministry: With an Inquiry into the Causes of Its Inefficiency* (Carlisle, PA: Banner of Truth, 1991), 361–83.

Reducing the sermon to the preaching outline that I will take into the pulpit comes next. I write the outline in the manuscript margins or on a separate piece of paper. If the weather permits, I walk around my neighborhood, giving more thought to the sermon delivery, meditation, and prayer.

How many hours do I spend preparing a sermon? I budget the same amount of time each week—about twenty hours for all my study in preparation for preaching and teaching, which includes Sunday school lessons, Bible studies, and school lectures. On individual sermons, I take as little time as I need to prepare a message that is faithful to the text and will edify the congregation. Preaching may be the preeminent work of the pastor, but it's not his only work. Sermons must be prepared efficiently.

Let me add a word about uploading your sermon audio to the Internet. Certainly, this can benefit your congregation by allowing those who miss the service to keep up with your series. But a word of caution: if concerns about smoothness of delivery and avoiding occasional grammatical and syntactical errors drive you to read your manuscript, think carefully. The people sitting in front of you are no longer your principal concern. Pride of product has trumped the passionate, earnest, and sometimes stumbling efforts that accompany earnest gospel preaching. You are a preacher, not a performer.

Pray for Yourself and Your Congregation

Prayer is a part of preparation at every point. Pray for God's grace to understand his infallible Word, for his grace to expound it with integrity and dependence on the Spirit, and for his grace to the congregation, that they may receive the Word by faith. Sermon preparation constantly exposes your own sins, making the hours spent in the study a time of humble confession, repentance, and renewal.

Revise Your Sermon While You Preach

Be prepared to revise your sermon *while* you preach it! As I preach, things not on the paper come to my mind. Applications of the Word, illustrations, and other useful texts not previously thought of occur to me as I preach. Preaching is a creative act, and the imagination, sanctified by study and knowledge of the congregation's needs, should not be suppressed. What I actually preach varies (sometimes considerably) from what is in my manuscript and notes. We preach to real people, and as we see them and think of their needs, struggles, and burdens, we want to speak God's gracious Word to them.

Preach Earnestly

Your congregation must sense your depth of feeling—your affection for them and intense concern for their conversion and sanctification. Paul reminded the Ephesian elders, "I did not cease night or day to admonish every one with tears" (Acts 20:31). He wrote "out of much affliction and anguish of heart" to the troubled Corinthians, "with many tears" (2 Cor. 2:4). Your congregation must have your transparent solicitude for their spiritual well-being.

Preach Sympathetically

You are a sinner preaching to a congregation of sinners. As you experience disappointments, frustrations, and heart-aches in your own life, your sympathy for your congregation will grow. Mine has. Suffering is God's academy of sanctification, where he equips ministers to serve in the real world—the one broken by sin and filled with sorrows—not an ideal world beyond the reach of affliction and the pull of temptation.

Our Savior "learned obedience through what he suffered" (Heb. 5:8), and so will you as you know him and "the fellowship of his sufferings, being made conformable unto his death" (Phil. 3:10 KJV). Pulpit thunderings must give way to heartfelt tenderness.

Not every problem has a clear and absolute solution, nor every question a black-and-white answer. So be careful about offering three quick and easy steps to revitalizing your prayer life, strengthening your marriage, or being a peacemaker—advice that will only compound the anguish of broken and discouraged believers.

Appeal to Conscience

"By the open statement of the truth," Paul wrote to the Corinthians, "we would commend ourselves to everyone's conscience in the sight of God" (2 Cor. 4:2). The true minister pleads with his congregation to stop suppressing God's truth and to conform their thoughts, affections, and behavior to his revealed will. Through you, God appeals to the congregation: "Be reconciled to God" (2 Cor. 5:20)!

Be Patient with Yourself

I preached my first sermon when I was in my late teens. Only in my mid-thirties did I begin to preach sermons that I would later reuse with minor revisions. In my older sermons, I find occasional outlines, illustrations, paragraphs, or ideas that I want to use again, but that's about it. It took years for me to reach what I would call pulpit maturity.

Perhaps I matured more slowly than others. Still, I caution you not to set unrealistic expectations for your sermons early on. It takes time to cultivate the gifts and hone the skills that lead to pulpit maturity. True, there are pulpit prodigies, like Charles Spurgeon. But they are few in number. Thank God for them, but never make them the measure by which you judge your own preaching.

Take heart! Your sermon is God's Word preached, the divinely appointed means to gather, save, and build his church. Certainly, you want to handle God's Word carefully, so strive to prepare thoroughly and speak clearly. Nevertheless, even when you're unsatisfied and words don't come easily, God is at work. By his Spirit, he is applying his preached Word to the needs of his congregation. He will own your weak endeavors to secure his beloved people's growth in grace.

A Word to Ruling Elders

Wise ruling elders help a congregation learn how to receive God's Word from their ministers. They impress upon the congregation that "it is required of those that hear the Word preached, that they attend upon it with diligence, preparation, and prayer; examine what they hear by the Scriptures; receive the truth with faith, love, meekness, and readiness of mind, as the Word of God; meditate, and confer of it; hide it in their hearts, and bring forth the fruit of it in their lives."[4] Elders, be mindful that there is much you can do to prepare your congregation to support your new pastor and his ministry of the Word.

Faithful preachers make preaching a priority. So do faithful elders and faithful congregations. Together they grow in the grace and knowledge of our Lord Jesus Christ.

---

4. Westminster Larger Catechism 160.

"Far better no pulpit at all than a pulpit that did not, as its chief business, solemnly address men as lost sinners, summon them to repentance, faith, and humility, and entreat them, in Christ's stead, to be reconciled to God."

—WILLIAM G. BLAIKIE[5]

"Expository preaching consists in the explanation and application of a passage of Scripture. Without explanation it is not expository; without application it is not preaching."

—T. H. L. PARKER[6]

4

Practical Advice on Preaching

OBJECTIVE: To consider the right questions about preaching before you begin your pastorate.

ANSWERING BASIC QUESTIONS about ministry can keep you from common pitfalls and help you to get off to a good start in your new church.

How Long Should You Preach?

For most American congregations, twenty-five to thirty minutes of preaching is long enough. In churches committed to family worship, young children are sitting with their parents. Don't torture them. A service that goes beyond sixty to seventy-five minutes may not be realistic.

The length of the sermon is a question of both the congregation's capacity and your ability. Don't overestimate your skill at sustaining a congregation's interest. In my experience, lengthy sermons are often unnecessarily repetitive and laden with extraneous material. The result is a sermon without two fruits of discipline: a clear structure and focus.

In sermon preparation, what you exclude from your sermon is almost as important as what you include. Eliminate tedious background material. Capable students of the Word can unintentionally do damage here. They attempt to pack too much material into a sermon. As I have worked with ministerial candidates, I have become convinced that the discipline of estimating the length of a sermon is valuable. Here's why: you understandably want to share the fruits of your learning with your congregation, but the result can be information overload, or, in a rush to get the material out, points are not clearly established and connected.

My sermon manuscript seldom exceeds six typed pages. Before I work on my final draft, the sermon may run eight or nine pages. I ask myself: Is this point necessary? Am I needlessly repeating myself? Does that illustration really illumine the text or does it distract? Is this an important point, but one that would more clearly emerge in a later text? By disciplining myself to stay within realistic time limits, I'm not trying to eliminate spontaneity in the pulpit or adequate exposition of the text. I do attempt to make sure every point and every illustration has a purpose, while not taxing the listening capacity of my congregation.

When You Arrive at Your First Church, What Should You Preach First?

I almost always preach expository sermons through books of the Bible, interrupting that pattern only for sermons on the key redemptive-historical events that are embedded in the Western Christian calendar—Advent (Christ's first and second comings), Good Friday (the crucifixion), Easter (the resurrection), Ascension, and Pentecost.

Think about beginning with an epistle. In the history of redemption, these letters address believers in the situation that is most like ours: after the crucifixion, the resurrection, the

Ascension, and Pentecost, and awaiting Christ's coming again and the world to come. My first sermon series have come from Galatians, Ephesians, 1 Thessalonians, and 1 Peter.

I then move into an Old Testament book, followed by a gospel. Seldom do I vary from this rotation: Old Testament, gospel and Acts, and epistle. If members of my congregation attend morning and evening worship and Sunday school, then over the course of five or six years they will have spent time in every major literary category of the Bible: law, history, wisdom, prophecy, gospel, epistle, and apocalypse.

Expository sermons through books of the Bible will keep you from riding your own personal hobbyhorses—a style of preaching sure to promote controversy.

Once a preacher came to me for advice. His church was small and growing smaller. What should he do?

I am not a church-growth consultant. The only thing I could think to do was ask, "What are you preaching?" He said, "My congregation is not very Presbyterian, so my last two series have been on infant baptism and fencing the Lord's Table." His answers told me that issues that were important to him were the driving force behind his sermons. Pastors often preach through issues that are important to them in order to "fix" their congregations. That won't do.

On the other hand, if you address these issues as they arise in your preaching though books of the Bible, people will understand that you present biblical doctrines and their applications out of faithfulness to the text. Moreover, you will also be able to establish the canonical context for the truths your church confesses.

How Can Adult Sunday School Classes Complement Your Preaching?

If you take a church that has no adult educational program or one of poor quality, then your church's elders may look to you to fix the problem. Training an adult teacher takes time, especially if the depth of biblical knowledge and theology is poor. Also, the thought of adding yet another prep time to your schedule might seem overwhelming. One solution is to make adult Christian education a part of your preaching ministry. Use the Sunday school hour for questions about the sermon, and to explore issues that need more time to develop.

In one church that had multiple home groups that met during the week, I wrote study notes and questions built around the Sunday sermon. This extended the influence of my pulpit ministry, and it involved substantially less work than preparing a fresh lesson series.

Should You Speak to Political, Economic, and Scientific Controversies?

Ministers must speak only what they are competent to speak, and it is God who defines competence.

Young (and older) ministers should not preach on economics, scientific questions, or political controversies. I have heard sermons on why Christians should support the proposed B-1 bomber program (based on Nehemiah and his wall), the nature of Abraham Lincoln's Christian faith (he was an evangelical, I was assured), economics (the Bible is pro-capitalist and antisocialist—and vice versa), the age of the earth, and the meaning of the First Amendment's Establishment Clause. In each sermon, I judged the speaker to be addressing areas beyond his expertise. That's bad enough. But more disturbing, they addressed issues to which the Scriptures do not speak.

Edmund Burke, an eighteenth-century British statesman and Member of Parliament, warned:

> Politics and the pulpit are terms that have little agreement. No sound ought to be heard in the church but the healing voice of Christian charity. The cause of civil liberty and civil government gains as little as that of religion by this confusion of duties. Those who quit their proper character, to assume what does not belong to them, are, for the greater part, ignorant both of the character they leave, and of the character they assume. Wholly unacquainted with the world in which they are so fond of meddling, and inexperienced in all its affairs, on which they pronounce with so much confidence, they have nothing of politics but the passions they excite. Surely the church is a place where one day's truce ought to be allowed to the dissensions and animosities of mankind.[1]

Christians will have opinions about all sorts of political issues that are important to our nation, but about which the Word of God is silent. Therefore, his ministers have no authority to speak to them from the pulpit. Most of the time, when ministers speak on politics, they speak as amateurs. But embarrassing sermons by pastors out of their depth are not my primary concern. What matters is that God does not grant his church and ministers the competence necessary to speak to those issues. Even if the former chairman of the Joint Chiefs of Staff became a minister, he would have no competence to speak from the pulpit on issues of national security.

---

1. Edmund Burke, *Reflections on the Revolution in France* (New York: Oxford University Press, 1993), 11–12.

A pastor is God's shepherd, called to gather God's elect people into his pilgrim church, nourishing them and protecting them as they prepare for the world to come. His pulpit ministry should not stray from this singular task.

The minister must guard his flock by speaking to moral threats while, at the same time, avoiding legislative controversy. For example, a minister can and should condemn abortion as a violation of the sixth commandment, the unlawful destruction of human life created in God's image. But he must remain silent about specific pieces of legislation, with their inevitable compromises and caveats. He has no authority to speak as God's ambassador to the crafting of legislation. Let Christians in their own private vocations and interests work toward the greatest good possible.

Also, be careful not to wrongfully bind the consciences of your congregation's members, obligating them to attack social evils. When I was a boy in the rural South, it was the anti-liquor crusade. Other issues have taken its place. I have served as vice president of a crisis pregnancy center, but I do not think any believer is obligated to work in the pro-life movement or to ameliorate any of the myriad of social evils of the day. Let your members work out their commitments in these areas as they take into account their giftings, duties, and interests. For many, caring for their family, tending to their work, and attending public worship are all they can and should handle. Don't crush them with burdens they were never intended to bear.

A similar danger arises when we begin to sound like graduation speakers, promising the congregation that we can transform the culture, and even change the world, if we just pray more, give more, and witness more. This kind of preaching can stretch a congregation to its breaking point, leaving it stressed and exhausted. It also is a far cry from Paul's emphasis. In 1 Timothy 2:2, he encourages prayers for kings and those in high positions so that the members of the church "may lead a peaceful and quiet life, godly and dignified in every way."

Treat social media as an extension of your ministry. Don't stir needless political controversy by what you publish on your blog, Facebook, or Twitter. Why run the risk of alienating those you are called to shepherd? You are a pastor, not a controversialist.

How Will the Quality of Your Pastoral Care Affect Your Pulpit Ministry?

How you treat your congregation during the week—how you speak to them, how you speak about them, and how you serve them—will influence the way they receive your ministry.

When you're not in the pulpit, keep these traits in mind:

- *Be earnest.* Earnestly pursue the sanctification of your congregation, not only when you preach, but throughout the week. A shepherd's devotion to his flock should be transparent and evident to all.
- *Be patient.* Know that however difficult it is for you to adjust to life with your congregation, the feeling is mutual. Your congregation must learn to live with you and your sins, weaknesses, and idiosyncrasies, and you with theirs. So be patient. If you become impatient with your congregation, arrogant and insisting on your own way, then you will construct a barrier that your pulpit ministry may not overcome. That is not Christ's way. "Love is patient and kind; love does not envy or boast; it is not arrogant or rude. It does not insist on its own way; it is not irritable or resentful" (1 Cor. 13:4–5).
- *Be affectionate.* Whether publicly or privately, speak of

your flock as people you cherish. After all, God cherishes them—and so should you. Affection has a proper place in ministry, doesn't it? Pastor Paul assured his beloved church at Thessalonica that he and his colleagues "were gentle among you, like a nursing mother taking care of her own children. So, being affectionately desirous of you, we were ready to share with you not only the gospel of God but also our own selves, because you had become very dear to us" (1 Thess. 2:7–8). If you deal with your congregation harshly or treat them as an imposition, they will struggle to receive your pulpit ministry.

Share the Word of God with your congregation and share your life with them. As you preach to a congregation you dearly love, they will see you, imperfect as you are, as an undershepherd, who takes his cues from the Great and Good Shepherd of the sheep. As you shepherd from the pulpit and in homes with earnestness, patience, and affection, your flock will become convinced that you, like your heavenly Father, are for them in Christ Jesus.

"Worship must above all serve the glory of God."

—HUGHES OLIPHANT OLD[7]

"Sing the Bible, pray the Bible, read the Bible, preach the Bible."

—LIGON DUNCAN[8]

"Ascribe to the LORD the glory due his name; worship the LORD in the splendor of holiness."

—PSALM 29:2

"God is spirit, and those who worship him must worship in spirit and truth."

—JOHN 4:24

"If, therefore, the whole church comes together and all speak in tongues, and outsiders or unbelievers enter, will they not say that you are out of your minds? But if all prophesy, and an unbeliever or outsider enters, he is convicted by all, he is called to account by all, the secrets of his heart are disclosed, and so, falling on his face, he will worship God and declare that God is really among you."

—1 CORINTHIANS 14:23–25

"Therefore let us be grateful for receiving a kingdom that cannot be shaken, and thus let us offer to God acceptable worship, with reverence and awe, for our God is a consuming fire."

—HEBREWS 12:28–29

5

Leading Worship

OBJECTIVE: To plan each part of your worship service—from the call to worship to the benediction—with a view to God's glory, the edification of the saints, and the gathering of the elect into Christ's church.

PLAN YOUR SERMONS. Just as importantly, plan your worship services.

What precedes and follows the sermon are God-commanded elements of worship. They are as integral as the proclamation of the Word, and must never be treated lightly. You and your people are summoned to worship God, and you must lead them. Lead them in the praises, petitions, and offerings prescribed by Scripture. You and your people are redeemed by grace. Nevertheless, you are still redeemed sinners. So with broken hearts, lead your brothers and sisters in confessions of sin, and with a joyful heart pronounce the Lord's declaration of forgiveness to the believing and repentant.

This chapter touches only briefly on the elements and order of worship. I will leave those essential matters to your seminary training and the many fine books that are available to pastors.[1]

---

1. If you are new to the Reformed tradition, these three books are a good place

My burden is to set forth practical matters that will assist you in preparing your own heart, and several realities to keep in mind as you plan and lead public worship.

Dignity

Lead your worship service with dignity. Silly banter, ill-prepared words, and a light and breezy manner have no place in Christian worship. I'm not advocating phony seriousness and a pseudo-reverential tone of voice, but a gravity befitting an assembly where the thrice-holy God dwells with his blood-bought people.

You must lead your congregation to worship God "with reverence and awe, for our God is a consuming fire" (Heb. 12:28–29). As the Word of truth is proclaimed, even the unbeliever should find "the secrets of his heart . . . disclosed" and conclude, "God is really among you" (1 Cor. 14:25).

The Service You Inherit

When you arrive at your first church, you will inherit an order of service. I advise leaving it unchanged for the time being, because folks become attached to their orders of worship, even those in need of reformation. Don't be in a hurry. If needed, change can come, but only after you have first persuaded your elders and then the congregation.

You may think I lack reformation zeal. Perhaps. But reformation of worship is a process that is never complete. Throughout your tenure, you will be working with your elders to bring your church's worship into closer conformity

---

to start: Old, *Worship: Reformed according to Scripture*; Ryken, Thomas, and Duncan, eds., *Give Praise to God*; and Terry L. Johnson, ed., *Leading in Worship*, rev. ed. (White Hall, WV: Tolle Lege Press, 2013).

to God's Word. If you attempt to move too quickly, people may either leave the church or be frustrated because they aren't prepared for change.

At first, you may not have the complete trust of your new congregation. That's understandable; trust takes time to develop. People are more likely to consider changes after you have won their confidence.

So take whatever order of service you have, and lead worship with godly diligence and dignity. Work hard at providing exemplary pastoral care. Build your relationship with the congregation first, and only then tackle the order of worship.

Length of Service

If you are committed to keeping children in worship and seated with their families, you will likely need to limit your service to sixty to seventy-five minutes. This means that decisions must be made about what is included and excluded.

The amount of music in evangelical worship services has increased during my lifetime. It is not uncommon to sing for fifteen or more minutes at the start of the service. The amount of singing affects the other parts of the service. Prayers, Scripture readings, and the sermon are given less time to make room for music. This is an unhealthy trade-off.

In one of my churches, some members wanted more time for singing in services than I thought prudent. I had no desire to quench their love for singing. Therefore, our elders decided to provide an extended time of singing *before* the start of the service. For some, this proved to be valuable preparation for worship. Others, especially those with young children, could arrive as the singing was winding down, without having missed the call to worship.

Psalm Singing

Each week I plan for the congregation to sing at least one selection from the Psalter. Although I do not believe that Christians are obligated to sing psalms exclusively, worship is impoverished without them. After all, on many occasions in the history of God's people, the Psalter was the only hymn-book, and generations were sustained as they sang the inspired Word of God. Your congregation will be strengthened, too.

Hymns and Songs

The best hymns take their cues from the psalms. As they are sung, believers adore God's character, praise him for his works of creation and redemption, express trust in the finished work of Christ, consider the sobering distinction between the righteous and the wicked, and exhort one another to covenant faithfulness in the midst of struggles, fears, and doubts.

Apart from its fidelity to Scripture, the most important requirement for a hymn is that the congregation be able to sing it with confidence. During your first year at a new church, work with your accompanist or music director to determine which hymns your congregation knows and sings well. This is especially important in smaller congregations. When numbers are small and your people can't sing the chosen hymns, a musical train wreck leaves everyone discouraged.

One new hymn every two months is plenty. When introducing new hymn tunes, have the accompanist or musicians play through an entire stanza once, so that people can hear the tune. If you have a choir or band, let it sing or play the hymn the previous week as an introit or offertory, and then sing or play the first stanza on the Sunday the hymn is introduced. The congregation can listen and then join in singing the first stanza again, followed by the remainder of the hymn. With a little forethought, you can help your congregation sing confidently.

Even if your congregation is comfortable with only a small number of hymns, you are in good shape. You can work to build its repertoire over time. If you think a song would enrich your congregation's worship, but they don't know the tune, substitute a well-known tune in the same meter. If you don't know what a hymn's meter is, ask your accompanist to explain.

Selecting Music

An able music director is a real plus. If he is skilled at coordinating hymns and other music with the themes of the worship service and your sermon, then he selects your hymns. That's one less task for you, and it fosters camaraderie and a relationship of mutual trust.

Reading the Scriptures

Include large amounts of Scripture in your worship services. If you don't, because you reason that people can read their Bibles at home, then you are probably overestimating the reading habits of your average member.

Recently I completed a two-year sermon series in Matthew. During that time, my Old Testament reading came from the book of Proverbs, and I read approximately half a chapter each week. Before the nonpreaching passage, I made comments based on the text that lasted about a minute. Obviously, my words were not a mini-sermon, but insights that would help listeners understand the meaning of the passage.

Frequently I also briefly introduce a hymn or Psalter selection before the congregation sings it.

During the week, practice reading the Scripture passages. On the value of Scripture passages read well, John Broadus writes:

> Good reading has an exegetical value, helping to make plain the sense. It also brings out the full interest, and impressiveness, of the passage read. There are passages which have had a new meaning for us, and an added sweetness, ever since we once heard them read, long ago, by a good reader.[2]

How much Scripture should you read? There is no fixed rule. Take into account the capacity of your congregation and decide.

As you pray for your congregation year after year, ask God to give them a hunger for his Word.

Pulpit Prayers

In prayer, you should pour out your heart to God as you lead your congregation. Therefore, I do not recommend reading your prayers. Freedom is forfeited. And inasmuch as you are an example for your congregation, you model how to pray. Your congregation will not write out their prayers before offering them to God. Neither should you.

Still, you must prepare to pray. In advance, think about the subject matter of your prayers. Vary the topics of your prayers and the portions of Scripture upon which they are based. This will keep your prayers from becoming routine and predictable.

The best preparation for pulpit prayer is a robust life of private prayer. As you pray over the passages you read in your

---

2. John A. Broadus, *On the Preparation and Delivery of Sermons* (Vestavia Hills, AL: Solid Ground Christian Books, 2005), 517.

study and make the language of Scripture the language of your prayers, you will find yourself more and more ready to lead your congregation in prayer.

A worship service includes several major categories of prayer: invocation, confession of sin, thanksgiving, intercession, prayer for illumination of the Scripture reading, and communion prayers. During the week, mull over in your mind how you will approach these prayers on the Lord's Day. There are many valuable resources to help you think about your pulpit prayers.[3]

Where to Place Announcements

Announcements should be brief. In some congregations, they take on a life of their own and have the feel of a revival service: detailed descriptions of events, the blessings of attendance, the afflictions of neglect, and a passionate invitation, for whosoever will, to come.

At other times, announcements are delivered like a sales pitch. Product benefits are outlined and objections overcome. Somewhere along the way, the reason for worship is lost.

Think about how to handle announcements. Mine go in one of two places: either before the start of the service or before the prayer of intercession. No more than one or two are mentioned. They last fewer than twenty seconds, about the time it takes to direct people to the appropriate information in the bulletin.

3. See Arthur Bennett, *The Valley of Vision* (Carlisle, PA: Banner of Truth, 2003); D. A. Carson, *A Call to Spiritual Reformation: Priorities from Paul and His Prayers* (Grand Rapids: Baker, 1992); Hughes Oliphant Old, *Leading in Prayer: A Workbook for Ministers* (Grand Rapids: Eerdmans, 1995); Matthew Henry, *A Way to Pray*, ed. O. Palmer Robertson (Carlisle, PA: Banner of Truth, 2010); and Terry L. Johnson, ed., *Leading in Worship*, rev. ed. (White Hall, WV: Tolle Lege Press, 2013).

When the announcements are mentioned before the prayer of intercession, it's because I intend to pray for what's announced. For example, if it's the start of the new Sunday school quarter, I'll pray that students and teachers will grow together in their understanding of God's Word.

A caution about announcements: they are not a substitute for one-on-one personal appeals. For example, at several of my churches, I have started annual missions conferences. Announcements are placed in the bulletin, but I don't rely on them to bring people out. With the church directory in hand, I call each family by phone and invite them to attend. You may think that's a lot of work. It is, but the outcome is worth it.

Once a group of deacons were frustrated that few men showed up to help out on workdays. So I called each man in the church and asked him to bring a specific tool or piece of equipment. A record turnout followed.

Announcements are helpful, but don't rely on them alone.

What about Children's Sermons and Children's Church?

Children's sermons and children's church unnecessarily lengthen the service, and more importantly, they communicate to children that the "other" sermon is not for them. At one of my churches, the elders decided (after much prayer and discussion over a period of months) to eliminate the children's sermons, along with children's church. Concerns that there would be a falloff in attendance among families with young children proved unfounded. In fact, attendance increased as young families continued to join the church. Serious Christian parents want their children to be in serious services of worship.

If the church has these when you arrive and you would prefer that they be eliminated, move slowly. Seldom should change be rushed. Take time to talk through the issues with your elders, and if they come on board, spend even more time talking face-to-face with parents. This type of change is not something to be sprung on people by email. If you cannot persuade your elders, don't sulk, but get on with ministry. Don't fight with your elders.

Sunday Evening Worship

Sunday evening worship has been a vital part of my sanctification of the Lord's Day. Because the day begins and ends in worship, it helps me to keep the holy character of the day throughout. That's one reason that the decision of many congregations to abandon the evening service saddens me.

If your church has a Sunday evening service, attendance might be small compared to the morning service. My advice is to continue the service and make the case to the congregation for its value. Give the service your best effort! Work just as hard to plan the evening service as you do the morning service. By your behavior, tell your people why you cherish the evening service. If you approach it indifferently, then don't expect your congregation to take the service seriously.

In one congregation, the Sunday evening service was very small. The service was led from a lectern placed in front of a piano in the corner of the sanctuary. The preachers wore suits on Sunday morning, but dressed casually for the evening service.

My response was to preach from the center of the sanctuary, as if I actually expected people to show up. I dressed as I did on Sunday morning and expended as much energy in preparing and leading the evening service as the other. Attendance began to increase. If you act like you expect few to come, then few will come. Instead, set your expectations high.

I do shorten the evening service. It seldom lasts more than fifty minutes. Parents are bringing their children, who may be tired at the end of the day and may need to be up early for school the next day. Marathon evening services are counter-productive. Encouraging moms and dads to persevere in sanctifying the entire day is on my mind, and an evening service of reasonable length helps.

Preparing the Bulletin

My staff's time is valuable. Getting bulletin information late to my accompanists and office manager makes their lives unnecessarily hectic. So I get information to them well in advance, ordinarily at least seven to ten days before the service. For new musicians, who are learning the ropes of accompanying congregational singing, having the hymn and Psalter selections early permits ample time for practice.

On Wednesday or Thursday, my assistant sends electronically to the congregation the bulletin for the upcoming Lord's Day. Some parents incorporate the hymns into their family worship, so that the children are familiar with them before they arrive. Parents can explain difficult words and talk about the themes of the hymns. Scriptures can be read in advance and taught.

Janitorial and Security Staff

Getting the church ready for Sunday worship often involves a cleaning crew and security officers. If you hire people from outside your church, by all means learn their names. Inquire about their families. Pray with them when they face crises. Attend visitations and funerals. When non-church members work for your congregation, they are part of the family. Treat them with love and respect. If they are unbelievers, they are potential brothers and sisters in Christ.

Conclusion

Nail down your theology of worship before you arrive at your first church. But remember, you will have to make many decisions about practical issues from the start.

"Q. 92. What is a sacrament?

"A. A sacrament is a holy ordinance instituted by Christ; wherein, by sensible signs, Christ, and the benefits of the new covenant, are represented, sealed, and applied to believers.

"Q. 93. Which are the sacraments of the New Testament?

"A. The sacraments of the New Testament are, baptism, and the Lord's Supper."[9]

—WESTMINSTER SHORTER CATECHISM

"Go therefore and make disciples of all nations, baptizing them in the name of the Father and of the Son and of the Holy Spirit."

—MATTHEW 28:19

"Repent and be baptized every one of you in the name of Jesus Christ for the forgiveness of your sins, and you will receive the gift of the Holy Spirit."

—ACTS 2:38

"Do you not know that all of us who have been baptized into Christ Jesus were baptized into his death? We were buried therefore with him by baptism into death, in order that, just as Christ was raised from the dead by the glory of the Father, we too might walk in newness of life."

—ROMANS 6:3–4

"For I received from the Lord what I also delivered to you, that the Lord Jesus on the night when he was betrayed took bread, and when he had given thanks, he broke it, and said, 'This is my body, which is for you. Do this in remembrance of me.' In the same way also he took the cup, after supper, saying, 'This cup is the new covenant in my blood. Do this, as often as you drink it, in remembrance of me.' For as often as you eat this bread and drink the cup, you proclaim the Lord's death until he comes."

—1 CORINTHIANS 11:23–26

6

The Sacraments

OBJECTIVE: Before you administer baptism or the Lord's Supper, to think through both their spiritual significance and the practical issues you may face in your new congregation.

YOU ARE A minister of the Word and sacraments. In your first church, you will have the solemn duty and great joy of administering the two sacraments that Christ has given his church—baptism and the Lord's Supper.

The ministry of the Word presents Christ and his benefits to the ear, and the sacraments present them to the eye. Wherever the Word is faithfully preached and heard and the sacraments are rightly administered, you will find a praying pastor, one who asks the Lord to bless his ministry of the Word and sacraments to the nourishment of the souls for whom Christ died.

The sacraments should never be administered apart from the ministry of the Word. It is the preached Word that declares their significance and sets the water, bread, and wine apart from common use. That is why in historic Protestant architecture, the baptismal font and the communion table are placed in front of the sanctuary and under the pulpit. Apart from the Word, they are without spiritual meaning.

I assume you have read your denomination's confessional statements and its book of church order. Because they establish the doctrine and practice of your denomination, you must adhere to them closely. Your ordination vows bind you in the Lord to uphold the teachings of your denomination.

The advice that follows is meant to help you with a few practical issues that will arise as you administer baptism and the Lord's Supper.

Baptism

Instituted by Christ, baptism belongs in the church's public service of worship. Ministers should never administer baptism in private ceremonies.

On some occasions, baptism must be administered outside the Lord's Day assembly. A new believer may be too sick to attend worship, and there may be little hope of his recovery. Or someone has come to faith while serving a lengthy prison sentence. In these situations, the church, at the direction of its elders, is called to worship at bedside or in a jail cell. The number of those able or permitted to gather may be few. Nevertheless, it is the church that gathers to worship.

The relationship between the minister and his fellow elders should not be overlooked. A minister is not an independent religious worker or spiritual lone ranger who makes the decision to baptize or not to baptize. His authority comes from Christ, who has called him through the church to minister to the church. As a colaborer with others whom God has called, he governs in the church as one elder among several. Collectively, elders interview those desiring baptism to determine whether they give credible evidence of faith and repentance.

Baptism is not the work of the minister or of the person baptized. It is the work of the risen and ascended Christ, who has called, regenerated, and given the gifts of faith and repentance to the new believer. It is the Savior who has washed the new believer with his blood, which the washing with water signifies. At Christ's command, the minister places the name of the triune God upon the believer: "I baptize you in the *name* of the Father, and of the Son, and of the Holy Spirit."

The focal point of baptism is not the new believer's profession of faith and promise of obedience, but God's promise of salvation to his people.

Now to practical matters.

Know your congregation's traditions. Before your first baptism, determine whether there is a special tradition at baptisms. Some congregations sing the doxology or "Children of the Heavenly Father" or a stanza of "Jesus Loves Me" after baptisms. Don't needlessly offend by neglecting a cherished part of your congregation's history. Show respect for what has been previously practiced.

Place the baptism early in the liturgy. In my denomination, ministers baptize new believers upon profession of faith in Christ *and* their children. If you are baptizing an infant or young child, place the baptism early in the service. In services that I lead, baptism immediately follows the call to worship, opening hymn, invocation, and confession of faith. Keep to a minimum the amount of time parents must wait with their often-restless children.

Don't make baptism a trial for the parents. I have seen the baptism placed right before or even after the sermon. Agitated and crying children are brought to the front of the church in the arms of distraught parents. Don't detract from the joy of the day by making it a religious marathon for parents and children.

Be brief. When providing the scriptural warrants for baptism, be clear and brief. A baptismal service is not the place for a lengthy exposition of the nature of baptism. Reserve extended teaching on baptism for another time. I include detailed instructions on baptism when it is part of a text I am expounding, in inquirers' classes for those seeking church membership, and in Sunday school or catechism classes. When I visit with parents before the baptism of their first child, I review what the Bible teaches about baptism and the baptismal vows they will take.

Think carefully about what you will say before administering the sacrament. My remarks take approximately three minutes. Ordinarily, I review one biblical warrant for infant baptism. In some churches, baptisms occur regularly throughout the year. The frequency of baptism gives opportunities to supply biblical reasons for baptism and its duties. Don't overteach, especially if the parents are standing in front of you, child in arms.

Don't be polemical. If your church practices infant baptism, don't launch a diatribe against your Baptist brethren. Baptism of a child, not theological controversy, is the order of the day. State concisely and irenically why your church baptizes infants. Don't thoughtlessly offend guests of the family by mounting an assault on their views on baptism. A child's baptism should be a joyous time.

Be personal. Don't say the same thing at each baptism. Choose words that personalize. For example, if new believers are being baptized, share with the congregation how they came to faith in Christ.

If an adopted infant is being baptized, I may speak to the child (parents can let him know what I said later in life), reminding him that the most important decisions in his life are those made for him. I say to him: "None of us chooses our family. That decision is made for us. That is true of all children, but is especially clear when a child, like you, is adopted. This family has chosen to place its name upon you. Because your mom and dad are believers, you have a place in the church family and the name of the triune God is placed upon you. With your baptism comes great responsibility, none of which is more important than for you to confess your faith in the Savior, Jesus Christ." And as the child grows older, I'll remind him often of that responsibility.

Keep your sense of humor. You will need it. Children fuss. One toddler grabbed my lapel mic; another swiped my glasses. The four-year-old son of a new Christian kicked me in the shin, much to the horror of his mother. I'm not sure that it's funny, but I once unknowingly baptized an adult under his criminal alias. Things don't always go as planned; roll with the punches.

A baptism should fill a church with godly happiness. Therefore, look happy, smile, and speak affectionately. Along with the congregation, share the joy that men and women, and boys and girls, are baptized in the name of the Father, and of the Son, and of the Holy Spirit.

The Lord's Supper

Coming to the Lord's Table is a beautiful part of the service of worship! There the Holy Spirit raises believers' hearts to heavenly places and seats them with Christ, at the right hand of the Father. There they feed upon him by faith with thanksgiving.

Be familiar with your church's practices. As with baptism, it's important to understand your church's practices. Unfortunately, it is unlikely that you will have previously seen the Supper served at your new church. Traditions vary from church to church. Therefore, talk with the elders and make sure you understand the order. For example, some eat the bread and drink from the cup individually as the elements are passed. In other congregations, the congregation waits to eat and drink until everyone has been served. What is the practice at your new church? Where do your elders want you to sit when they serve you communion? Does the pianist play while the elements are served or is there silence? Is a special hymn sung before or after the sacrament?

Respect your new congregation by honoring its traditions. Later, you can recommend changes to your elders, but at the outset serve communion in the way that the church practiced it before your arrival.

Invitations and warnings. Before the administration of the elements, you will issue both an invitation and a warning.

Make the invitation earnest. Christ, the host of the meal, welcomes believers to his table. Invite them to eat the bread and drink the cup. This table is prepared for the Lord's sinful, frail, and frequently beleaguered people. Summon them to the nourishing feast that he provides.

Warn those who have not made a profession of faith or who have been suspended from the Table not to eat the bread or drink the cup, for in eating and drinking in an unworthy manner they bring judgment on themselves (1 Cor. 11:27–32). Be careful with your warning. Don't let its length or tone overwhelm the invitation that your dear and believing people need to hear. The gracious welcome of the Savior is paramount.

Some will not and should not receive the bread and wine. Those who are unbelievers or who are living scandalously or have not yet publicly professed faith in Christ may not come to the Table. Make sure that those who cannot partake of the Lord's Supper know that you are glad they are there. We do not ask them to leave the service. Without taking, they must let the bread and cup pass by. But urge them to take Christ as their Savior. Let them know that you desire their profession of faith and repentance, so that they might join in the Lord's holy meal.

Prepare. We should never approach the Lord's Table carelessly or administer the sacrament perfunctorily. Just as you would never preach a sermon without prayerful preparation, take time to plan this part of the worship service.

Think through your words of instruction, invitation, and warning carefully. I don't advise writing out your prayers, but you should give thought to them beforehand. Otherwise, your words become predictable and stale. Let the riches of the meal be reflected in your exhortations and prayers.

Be mindful of those who are unable to gather. Like baptism, the Lord's Supper is not a private affair. It is to be administered only in the public worship services of the church. You should decline invitations to serve the Supper to private groups or at weddings.

But what about those members who, because of infirmity, are no longer able to attend the church's worship services? The church must gather with them, so that they are not excluded from the ministry of Word and sacrament. In the churches I have served, the elders approve taking the Lord's Supper to shut-ins. These are not private services. As is appropriate, other members of the church body may gather. At one church, some women from the congregation and their daughters would come to the homes of elderly widows. They participated in the service, remaining after I left to enjoy fellowship with the shut-ins.

With a small gathering like this, I use an abbreviated order of service. I issue the call to worship, recite the Apostles' Creed, pray, offer a brief exposition of the previous Lord's Day text, and administer the sacrament. Again, I am leading a public, albeit shortened, worship service in the home of a shut-in.

Conclusion. You are a minister of the Word *and* sacraments. Give as much study, forethought, prayer, and care to administering the sacraments as you do to the proclamation of the Word of God. Christ's blood-bought people deserve nothing less.

"But all things should be done decently and in order."
—1 CORINTHIANS 14:40

"This is why I left you in Crete, so that you might put what remained into order."
—TITUS 1:5

7

Church Administration

OBJECTIVE: To acquire the mental disciplines, work habits, and organizational skills necessary for the growth and care of your first church.

CHURCH ADMINISTRATION. YAWN.

Frequently pulpit search committees rank administration low on the list of qualifications they seek in their next pastor. "We want a man who can preach and teach and visit and evangelize, but management skills aren't nearly as important." That's not true! Church administration is a skill that goes undervalued *until* it becomes conspicuous by its absence. Count on it: you will be held responsible for being a capable administrator—and you should be.

A careless attitude toward administrative matters indicates not deep spirituality, but indifference to the well-being of God's flock. Poor administration is the enemy of everything that you and your church value most. Without sound organization, your preaching and teaching will be uneven, your visitation haphazard, and your evangelistic work uncoordinated. Church administration demands your attention.

If you're still not persuaded of the importance of church administration, ask a wife whose husband mismanages family affairs or an employee laboring under incompetent leaders how important sound management is. You'll get an earful. Like families and businesses, churches wither and anger builds under poor management.

To be sure, don't expect to be rewarded for competent administration. Do expect, however, a tumultuous pastoral tenure if you fail to guide the congregation with a steady hand.

Mercifully, administration is a skill you can learn. Let's cover the basics.

Get a Grip on Your Calendar

Let me suggest how to start your day: First, do your devotions. Second, look at your calendar. And how to end your day: First, look at your calendar. Second, say your prayers. Keep close to your calendar. Missed or tardy appointments and showing up unprepared for meetings reflect poorly on you and the church you represent.

What goes on your calendar? All appointments and work due. I encourage seminary students to take their class syllabi and put on their calendar class schedules, exam dates, and what work is due on which days. Forgetting an assignment is not an indication of poor memory, but of calendar carelessness. The disciplined use of a calendar must carry over from seminary into the pastorate.

Get a Grip on Your Church's Calendar

Think ahead. I plan conferences eighteen to thirty-six months ahead of time. Speakers have to be invited, and if your church doesn't have a building, venues must be arranged.

Think about church programs. Take Sunday school as an example. Does the new Sunday school year begin in August?

Then you will want to have all preparatory work completed before summer begins. Late winter and early spring is the time of year to finalize details for the coming Sunday school year. Wait until the last minute, and you will find that top teachers are no longer available, new recruits are thrown into classes unprepared, curriculum arrives late, students are bored, and no one is happy.

Be thorough. Identify your goal—in this case, the start of Sunday school—and build into your calendar everything you need to reach the goal—teacher recruitment, teacher training sessions, the ordering of curriculum, and visits to key people to persuade them of the importance of Christian education.

As your church grows, you will be able to recruit a leader to assume this responsibility. But as your ministry gets under way, the responsibility may fall to you. The best way to equip a volunteer to take over any responsibility is to show him how to do the job right.

Get a Grip on Meetings

Choose carefully the meetings you attend. Your first church may have regular elders', deacons', and committee meetings. If you attend all of them, you will find yourself out several evenings a month. Add those nights to Sunday evening worship and midweek Bible study/prayer meeting (fixtures in many churches), and you're out a lot—away from your family and expending nights that could be used to visit prospective members.

Many pastors begin their ministries in churches that are small or declining or both. Church growth in these congregations requires the pastor's leadership, and that means making time for getting together with potential members. Some of this can be done over breakfasts and lunches with men, but evening visitation, especially of families, will be necessary. The pastor committed to attending every church meeting will find himself working against the growth of his church.

Not everyone will or should adopt my solution, but from the start of my ministry it has been this: I regularly attend only elders' meetings. Periodically, my presence may be needed at other meetings, but I keep the number to a minimum. Sometimes committees need my help to retool for their work or to recruit and train a leader, but most of the time they can function without me. In a small or declining church, the one person whose involvement is critical in reaching potential new members is you. Don't let other responsibilities keep you from it.

Prepare Agendas for Most Meetings You Do Attend

Of course, there are meetings for which I prepare no agenda. Appointments are made each week just to be with people, to share their company and to talk about the things of the Lord. It's how you get to know a congregation, build friendships, and understand people's cares, concerns, and joys.

But for all other meetings, I come with an agenda. Often it involves jotting down items that need to be discussed or questions I have. My members' time is precious, and my memory is porous, so I record in advance what needs to be discussed.

What is true of private meetings is especially true of board and committee meetings. Don't work without an agenda.

During my years in ministry, comparatively few of my elders' meetings have exceeded two hours. One reason for this is preparation. Ten days before a meeting, I email the elders a draft agenda and request from them items they want to be included on the final agenda. At least four days before the meeting, I email the final agenda, along with financial reports.

Here is a sample agenda:

Stated Monthly Session Meeting
First Presbyterian Church
September 16, 2016
6 P.M. (Conference Room)

FINAL AGENDA
1. Declaration of Quorum, Call to Order, and Opening Prayer (Pastor)
2. Prayer for the Congregation
3. Approval of 8/19/16 Minutes (Chalmers, see attachment)
4. Financial Reports (Candlish, see attached P&L and Balance Sheet)
5. Missions (Duff)
6. Education (Begg)
7. Church Discipline (Knox)
8. Additional Business
    a. Communication 1: Requests for letters of transfer (Chalmers)
    b. Communication 2: Request for hurricane relief gifts (Chalmers)
    c. December Holiday Schedule (Pastor)
    d. Etc.
    e. Etc.
9. Date and Time of Next Meeting: October 21, 2016, at 6 P.M.
10. Adjournment and Closing Prayer

Note these things about this agenda:

- Prayer for the congregation comes first. There are two reasons for this: (1) Elders will come prepared to pray for those in their shepherding group, and so the agenda items promote elder accountability. (b) The best time of the meeting, when the elders are relatively fresh and alert, is given to prayer for the congregation.

- At the end of each report, an elder prays for the matters and persons discussed. This creates an atmosphere of prayer.
- Stated meetings are scheduled late in the month, so that financial reports can be included.
- In order to avoid confusion, the elder responsible for each agenda item is identified by name.
- Printing the agenda and related materials in advance allows routine questions to be asked and answered before the meeting.

Be Sensitive to Time

You owe your board members efficient meetings. You can nap before the meeting or sleep in late after a lengthy meeting the previous night. Your elders can't. You owe them a meeting that stays on track.

Time sensitivity means eliminating unnecessary meetings. Through the years, I have discovered that my elders can conduct their business in nine meetings. So unless there is an emergency, no meetings are scheduled for December, June, and July. The congregation needs constant care, but elders do not need to be constantly meeting. Give them breaks.

Read Financial Reports Carefully

Read financial reports thoroughly, well before the meeting, and understand the contents. Identify potential trouble spots and head them off.

Example: On a February financial report, you discover that your Sunday school director has already spent 80 percent of her annual budget.

Scenario 1: You don't read the report in advance and show up clueless. "Why has Mrs. Smith spent almost her entire budget?" someone asks. For the next thirty minutes, elders vent their frustrations. The board's financial hawks (men you should love and appreciate) are eyeing you. After all, this fiscal fiasco is your responsibility.

Scenario 2: You read the report in advance and get the facts. (Don't miss that: get the facts!) You call your Sunday school director and discover that she has purchased the Sunday school materials for the entire year. It will help her review content and assist with teacher training. You also discover that she contacted the church treasurer in advance and obtained his approval before making the purchase. When you email the agenda in advance, you include this information. The meeting comes, and there are no surprises. The financial report is received without comment. All is well.

Get a Grip on Your Email

When someone says that he needs my help getting organized, this is where our conversation begins: "How many emails are currently in your in-box?"

"Let me check," he says, opening his computer. "1,509."

"Okay, let's start here."

Email is a useful tool for communicating information—meeting requests, read-aheads, prayer concerns, and the like. But it becomes a tyrant when it swells with news feeds and advertising or becomes a substitute for discussion and conversation that should belong to in-person or phone exchanges.

Borrowing and adapting ideas from David Allen,[1] I suggest checking email two or three times a day. Turn off distracting alarms. There's no good reason to look at your email every five minutes.

Keep an empty in-box. When I check email, I set aside time to give it my full attention. If an email can be dealt with in less than two minutes, I respond immediately. Most of the time, deleted emails are not filed by category, but go into a searchable file and can be recovered as needed.

All other emails go into one of three files:

A-File. Time-sensitive emails that cannot be dealt with in two minutes are placed in this file, and I return to them at the end of the day. Into my A-file go missionary prayer letters, so that I can read and pray with care.

B-File. Project emails are placed in my B-file, or are attached to the appropriate project management file in Evernote. Emails that require lengthy responses or additional information are placed here, too. Deadline alerts are set.

C-File. My C-file contains emails with reading materials that do not require a response.

I recommend deleting all news feeds except the ones you actually read. In deciding whether to remain on a distribution list, ask yourself: How much time do I spend reading news each day? Is it disproportionately high, compared to the time I spend reading while preparing for sermons and reading high-value books? I subscribe to only a handful of feeds.

Get rid of clutter that distracts from important emails.

---

1. David Allen, *Getting Things Done: The Art of Stress-Free Productivity* (New York: Penguin, 2001), 31–35. I read a book on time management and organization every few years. Some specifics in my system may have been inspired by other readings, but the sources are long forgotten.

Delegate Because It's Important to Work *with* People and Not Alone

Delegation is not only a matter of stewardship of your time; it also cultivates collegiality in churches dependent on volunteers. Delegation should be about team building. Work to create a culture where people pitch in and work together. Think of creative ways to involve your congregation. Don't be a loner; learn to love your team.

For example:

- In churches that lack office staff, I ask capable people to help prepare bulletins, letters, mailings, etc.—even though I am quite able to do those things myself. These helpers ease my burden and become partners in ministry.
- Ask health care professionals in your congregation who are routinely at hospitals to be part of your visitation team. Are they willing to visit for a few minutes with hospitalized members and visitors? Just as you strive to bring the comfort of the gospel to the sick, these Christian professionals can be a reassuring presence to your suffering people. Together you will provide a level of care that you could not reach alone.
- When one of my members goes to the hospital, my office manager immediately locates an elder and a deacon who will agree to visit or call. This creates teamwork as well as a culture of responsiveness.
- Ask welcoming and hospitable people to contact those new to your fellowship and community, to extend a welcome from your church, and to take them a meal. I love to visit with new people, but it is even better to include others from your church family.

Thank your people sincerely and often. Let them know how much you appreciate their concern for you and for the work of Christ's church.

Remember names. Wherever I go, my pocket notebook goes with me. As I meet people, I write down their names. Later I review them and commit them to memory. That's my system for recalling names. With a little effort, you can learn to greet people by name. If you pray for church visitors by name during the week, you can greet them by name when they show up. As you learn about their needs, you will be able to pray for them by name.

Use Social Media Sparingly

My personal rule for social media is simple: it is an extension of my ministry. If information does not advance the work of my church or seminary, I do not post it on my blog, Facebook, or Twitter.

My posts tend to fall into two categories: events of church and school, and celebrating the achievements of the people I serve.

What about matters of political controversy? I assume that the world does not need my opinion about political candidates or public policy. I gladly leave that to others.

My personal opinions are best shared in private, if at all. Why needlessly offend members or potential members of my church? If, for example, I endorse a candidate, why run the risk of alienating persons who will vote for the other candidate? Unlike some ministers and Christian celebrities, I don't think I can say of any man, "He is God's candidate."

Whether I like it or not, my social media will be judged to represent the churches I serve. They don't endorse candidates or issue public-policy statements, nor will I. If I were voicing my political beliefs on social media, readers might wrongly conclude that I speak for my church on these matters.

I do not deny that there are pressing moral issues that the church must think through. Abortion, the nature of marriage, racial justice, and poverty are just a few that come to mind. As these issues arise in Scripture, the minister must declare the mind of God from the pulpit.

But the crafting of legislation and public-policy solutions is not the work of the minister or the church. Forums can be established by concerned and competent Christians to help believers understand and think through complex issues. Often, even when Christians agree on the problem, they disagree on public-policy solutions. The pastor can do more good by pointing people to forums that host reasonable and informed debate than he can by wading into controversy himself.

Additional thoughts about social media:

- Too often pastors address complex issues about which they have no competence to speak. They embarrass themselves and their churches.
- I steer clear of theological controversy. Comments on Facebook do not lend themselves to thoughtful discussion—the kind I wish to promote.
- Many social media sites drive readership by trafficking in outrage and personal attacks—precisely the opposite of the climate that I want in my church.
- When I comment on someone else's Facebook page, it is ordinarily a congratulatory note or a word of encouragement or a promise of prayer. I want to build goodwill.
- Some pastors get into trouble with what they think are humorous posts. What they find humorous might needlessly offend members of their own congregation or

people we would like to see visit our congregation. So be careful.

- I am first and foremost a minister of the gospel. All else must be subordinated to that work, even my deeply held political and policy convictions.

Handle social media with extreme care.

Conclusion

Everyone benefits as you manage your first church well. Above all, the Lord is honored when you provide stable care for his precious people.

"Conflict provides opportunities to glorify God, to serve others, and to grow to be like Christ. . . . As you live out the gospel and make the Lord's priorities your priorities, you can turn every conflict into a stepping-stone to a closer relationship with God and a more fulfilling and fruitful Christian life."

—KEN SANDE[10]

"Behold, how good and pleasant it is when brothers dwell in unity!"

—PSALM 133:1

"Finally, brothers, rejoice. Aim for restoration, comfort one another, agree with one another, live in peace; and the God of love and peace will be with you."

—2 CORINTHIANS 13:11

"I therefore, a prisoner for the Lord, urge you to walk in a manner worthy of the calling to which you have been called, with all humility and gentleness, with patience, bearing with one another in love, eager to maintain the unity of the Spirit in the bond of peace."

—EPHESIANS 4:1-3

"And do not grieve the Holy Spirit of God, by whom you were sealed for the day of redemption. Let all bitterness and wrath and anger and clamor and slander be put away from you, along with all malice. Be kind to one another, tenderhearted, forgiving one another, as God in Christ forgave you. Therefore be imitators of God, as beloved children. And walk in love, as Christ loved us and gave himself up for us, a fragrant offering and sacrifice to God."

—EPHESIANS 4:30-5:2

"I entreat Euodia and I entreat Syntyche to agree in the Lord. Yes, I ask you also, true companion, help these women, who have labored side by side with me in the gospel together with Clement and the rest of my fellow workers, whose names are in the book of life."

—PHILIPPIANS 4:2-3

8

Growing through Conflict

OBJECTIVE: To learn to approach conflict as a means of sanctification for you and your congregation.

WHAT SANE PERSON enjoys conflict? Yet conflict can be a gift when we see what a large part it plays in our growth to maturity in Christ.

Yes, conflict is inescapable. Think otherwise, and your life and ministry will be miserable from misguided expectations.

And I am quick to add: if you delight in conflict, please get out of ministry now. A leader who thrives on stirring up controversy or looks forward to confrontation is nothing but a wrecking ball in the body of Christ.

One man who desired very much to be a leader in the church told me that he had the gifts of confrontation and rebuke. Given the strained relationships in every area of his life, I could well believe it! These are gifts that God's church can do without.

Here are three things that you must keep in mind when dealing with conflict:

First, although conflict is a painful part of life and ministry, the minister must maintain his bearing in controversy. He cannot afford to lose his poise. "Whoever is slow to anger is better than the mighty, and he who rules his spirit than he who takes a city" (Prov. 16:32). "The fruit of the Spirit is . . . self-control" (Gal. 5:22–23).

When you lose your poise and speak angrily or insensitively, your conscience will convict you. Confess quickly, agree with the Lord's verdict, and ask the forgiveness of all parties involved. Model biblical repentance when you have sinned.

I wish I could tell you I have never spoken angry words during my three decades of ministry, but I can't. What I can say is that I regret each and every one of them. Words can't be recalled. Whatever gratification comes from speaking them disappears almost immediately. But the harm they cause remains, and it can be dealt with only by confession and repentance.

Second, the leader must see conflict as a source of personal sanctification—and a source of peace and purity for the church.

What advantages come from conflict?

- Our personal sins are exposed. In conflict, heart anger, frustration, bitterness, and mistrust of God's providence quickly surface. The Lord is granting opportunities for us to repent and grow in conformity to Christ.
- Conflict reveals our limitations. In conflict, we find that we don't know the complete truth, that we need more information, that our initial judgments are often wrong, and that our cherished solutions aren't always the best.
- Doctrinal controversy can identify error and lead to its correction (Acts 15:1–31; Gal. 2:1–16). When the church contends with heresy, it provides an opportunity for the church to get back to its foundation, the Scriptures, and rediscover the power of truth. A stronger, more united church emerges from the heat of conflict.

- Church discipline involving false doctrine or scandalous behavior is never pleasant. But the result can be the restoration of the fallen to fellowship with God and his people (2 Cor. 2:5–11).
- Church discipline promotes the peace, purity, and reputation of the church by removing the unrepentantly immoral from the congregation (1 Cor. 5:1–13; 1 Tim. 1:18–20).

Third, solid relationships help to mitigate, prevent, and lessen conflict. I can't emphasize this too strongly. Good relationships are built over time, and as the bond of trust strengthens, you are less likely to have serious, long-term conflict. Trust is not a given. It must be earned and vigilantly protected.

Now let's give attention to attitudes and behaviors that will enable us to navigate conflict to the glory of God.

Learn to Overlook Offenses

"Good sense makes one slow to anger, and it is his glory to overlook an offense" (Prov. 19:11). Many things are irritating, but are not critical to the well-being of the church. Not every slight is intentional and meant to hurt you. Most differences of opinion have no long-term consequences. Some errors cannot be corrected. Figure out what's worth talking about and what's better to overlook. Don't risk conflict over things that are trivial and of little consequence.

Pray Comprehensively for Your Congregation

Praying comprehensively for your congregation means praying for more than the problems you face with individuals. Think about your flock and their many different relationships, occupations, trials, temptations, and needs—both physical and spiritual. Don't reduce your prayers to asking the Lord to overcome problems you have with people. Comprehensive intercessory prayer has the salutary effect of keeping the whole person in view, and keeps you from focusing only on strained relationships and gnawing on bones of contention.

Count the Number of Times You Encourage and Express Concern

When relationships are tense, we tend to avoid the persons with whom we are in conflict or talk only about what divides us. Take the initiative to be an encourager. Make sure you praise what is praiseworthy, encourage where you see evidences of grace, and speak words of compassion where needed. You want the number of these interactions to far exceed the number that are focused on controversy.

Measure in Advance the Effects of Your Words

When you must speak to a problem or express a concern, measure in advance the effects of your words. If you prize a reputation for being direct, think again. A tell-it-like-it-is attitude won't do. Mature leaders think carefully about how their words will be received. When dealing with controversy, bluntness is most often harmful. Be truthful, but don't state your position in a way that provokes hurt feelings or an angry and defensive response.

If your elder who is responsible for education presents you with his recommendation for the next year's Sunday school curriculum, you could be direct, saying, "I find this unacceptable. The lessons are moralistic, and their biblical foundation is weak to nonexistent." Or you could say, "Thank you for researching this. I know that took a lot of time. What did you find helpful about the curriculum? Do you have any concerns? Thank you for asking me to review it. May I express some strengths and weaknesses I see?" Be your leader's partner in serving. Talk through the issues.

Don't Attempt to Resolve Conflict by Email or Text

Two leaders had offices down the hall from each other. For months, they exchanged scores of emails as they argued over just about everything. They seldom spoke to each other, and their relationship was in tatters. It's too bad their computers weren't confiscated. Maybe then they would have talked face-to-face, saved the relationship, and spared others much hurt.

Emails are great for scheduling meetings and forwarding information. For resolving conflict, they are worthless. You cannot hear the tone of voice, see body language, and quickly clarify meaning or correct misunderstanding. During an email exchange, if you sense a personal problem emerging, pick up the phone and call. If necessary, plan to meet face-to-face.

Be Careful Whom You Imitate

During the last decade of the twentieth century, talk radio and cable news became staples of American life. I warned seminarians that if they adopted the angry tones and name-calling of prominent hosts, they would create division and drive away many of the people they should be striving to serve. This remains true today. Sarcasm, demeaning those with whom you disagree, and firing well-crafted zingers may drive ratings or elicit laughter, but they are incompatible with biblical ministry.

My own personal practice is to skip most talk radio and

cable news shows. Why imbibe the angry and divisive spirit of the age?

Take Potential Conflict off the Table

Classes for potential new members are a good place to lay out nonnegotiables. Nonnegotiables are those things upon which your church will not budge. These include matters of biblical principle and congregational priorities. They should be disclosed up front to those exploring membership in your congregation.

In one region of the country, many people visiting my church came from backgrounds where women were ordained to the biblical offices. My denomination doesn't do that. I informed each class that my congregation will not ordain women to the offices of elder and deacon, and gave reasons why. Frequently, questions came, each one appreciated and answered, hopefully with grace. Finally, I made it clear that our position is nonnegotiable, and that if anyone unites with our congregation while holding a contrary position, he should not expect the church to change. "I'm glad you're here," I said. "But if this is not an interpretation of the Bible you can live with, you will need to find another church home. And if you need my assistance, I'd be honored to sit down with you and discuss churches that might be a good fit."

The congregations I serve have a traditional order of worship, and those considering membership should not expect that to change. To pretend that change is a possibility is just that—pretending. That would be duplicitous and a false representation, bound to create ill will and conflict. Some pastors, desperate for new members, say things to raise expectations that will not be met. In doing so, they lay the groundwork for future controversy that could have been easily avoided.

At another congregation, we put our church school's need for a facility ahead of the congregation's desire for a sanctuary. Prospective members needed to understand that if they united with the church, it might mean worshiping in a gym for many years. If this was not an arrangement they could live with, they were advised to find another church home.

Speak winsomely. Explain why nonnegotiables will not change. Without defensiveness, accept criticism and answer questions patiently. Some will move on to other church homes. That's preferable to years of unhappy conflict. Others will be won over, either during the class or later on. Others will stay, not because they agree with you on every issue, but because they want to be in a church that understands its identity and presents its convictions irenically. In an age of conflict and angry words, a congregation at peace is attractive to those who want to worship and serve in peace.

Don't Demand the Last Word

In disagreement, give the other person the last word. Don't abuse your position of authority by taking final shots in a dispute. Don't try to force agreement. Give people space to think and return later for more conversation.

Serve, Serve, Serve . . . and Be Served

Through the years, I have had a number of substantial conflicts with leaders in my churches over such matters as the direction of a building campaign, the shape of a church discipline case, and the oversight of a school. In every case, decisions were made over extended periods, after considering various points of view. Not everyone was entirely happy with every decision. Often compromises were reached. Still, we stuck together.

Why? For many reasons, I suppose. Certainly, the leaders' devotion to the Lord and his church would top the list. But another factor that built a reservoir of goodwill was my involvement in their families' lives—visiting, performing weddings and funerals, attending award ceremonies, teaching their children, walking with them in troubled times—the routine stuff of pastoral ministry.

And my leaders have helped *me*—visiting me when I've been sick, offering encouragement, caring for my children, offering timely counsel, standing beside me in dark valleys—the routine stuff that good leaders do for their pastor.

Goodwill builds through the years, and helps to put disagreements in healthy perspective.

Serve your leaders. Let them serve you. And you will be well on your way to making church a place of trust, where conflict leads to your growth in sanctification and to peace and purity in the congregation you love.

"It belongs to the office of elder . . . to watch diligently over the flock committed to his charge, that no corruption of doctrine or of morals enter therein. . . . They should visit the people at their homes, especially the sick. They should instruct the ignorant, comfort the mourner, nourish and guard the children of the Church."[11]

—THE BOOK OF CHURCH ORDER OF THE PRESBYTERIAN CHURCH IN AMERICA

"I did not shrink from declaring to you anything that was profitable, and teaching you in public and from house to house."

—ACTS 20:20

"Religion that is pure and undefiled before God, the Father, is this: to visit orphans and widows in their affliction, and to keep oneself unstained from the world."

—JAMES 1:27

9

Home Visitation[1]

OBJECTIVE: To learn to make home visitation a vital part of your ministry.

WHEN YOU VISIT your flock, you bring the ministry of the Word to homes, hospitals, prisons, and any other place where people find themselves in need of a pastor's care. This chapter is focused on systematic home visitation.

Biblical pastors are shepherds. They know their sheep by name. They know their needs and, using the resources of God's Word, are ready to meet those needs with the compassionate skill that a true shepherd has for his sheep. Building on this biblical truth, the church has a long history of pastor and elder visitation in the homes of its members. W. G. T. Shedd stresses that

> a faithful and constant performance of the duty of pastoral visiting, is a means of grace. No one who has had any experience in this respect, will deny this for a moment. There is nothing better adapted to develop piety, to elicit the latent

1. Much of the contents of this chapter first appeared in a 1995 article I wrote for *New Horizons in the Orthodox Presbyterian Church*, and it is reprinted here with permission.

principles of the Christian, than going from house to house, and conversing with all varieties of character, and all grades of intelligence upon the subject of religion.[2]

I grew up in a Presbyterian tradition where home visitation was a regular part of the pastor's work. I had several role models. Many seminarians don't. Some have never received a visit from a pastor. So let's review the basics.

Home Visitation: What It Is Not

Systematic home visitation is not a hospitality service. Elsewhere I argue that hospitality is an essential discipline in healthy churches.[3] But as important as it is, hospitality is not the goal of pastoral visitation.

Systematic home visitation is not a counseling service. From time to time, members of the church have great needs that require counsel from mature and experienced pastors and elders. These needs might be discovered while visiting in a home. However, the purpose of home visitation is not counseling.

Systematic home visitation is not a social visit. Chatting about sports, current events, and the weather help to put people at ease with each other and build relationships. But home visits are not social calls.

Home Visitation: What It Is

Systematic home visitation fosters the spiritual growth of your church's members by assisting them in living disciplined Christian lives. Personal and family growth require

2. William G. T. Shedd, *Homiletics and Pastoral Theology* (New York: Charles Scribner's Sons, 1902), 343.
3. See chapter 10.

a commitment to key spiritual disciplines, such as prayer, Bible study, and worship. Home visits should cultivate those disciplines.

But you ask, "How will people react if I come to discuss spiritual matters?" Admittedly, they may be uncomfortable initially, especially if it has not been a part of your new church's history. And you may be uncomfortable, too! But home visitation serves a purpose so vital that it must not be neglected.

Before you become too anxious about how members will respond, remember that they were already asked probing questions about spiritual matters when they prepared to take their membership vows. (I assume here that you and your elders interview candidates before membership, and that you delve into evidences of faith in Jesus Christ and true repentance.) Pastoral visits build on that work.

If you are introducing systematic home visitation to your congregation, some of your members may not be comfortable with direct questions about their spiritual condition. But because of their membership interviews, they do have at least limited experience with it. Build on what your church leaders began when they asked questions about the members' faith. Make concern for their spiritual progress a way of life.

Other members will assume that when pastors visit, they come concerned about the condition of their souls. Why disappoint them? If people expect pastors to discuss spiritual matters, let's meet their expectations.

How to Schedule a Home Visit

Home visits should always be scheduled. Unless it's an emergency, unannounced visits are rude. I recommend scheduling by phone or email. A phone call might go like this: "Jan, I will be making pastoral visits next Thursday evening. Might I stop by and see you and Steve at seven o'clock for about forty-five minutes?" The purpose of the phone call is to arrange a visit and to assure the couple that you won't camp out in their living room for the evening. You might also schedule two or three visits the same evening.

What to Ask

After the usual exchange of pleasantries, it is good to remind people that you and the elders of the church are servants. You might say, "Thank you for welcoming me into your home. As you know, our church's elders are concerned that our members are growing in the Christian life. I am grateful for the opportunity we have tonight to discuss your family's walk with the Lord. So let me begin by asking . . ."

You could ask questions like this:

- In what ways are you growing as a disciple of Christ?
- What difficulties are you facing? How can we assist you in meeting them?
- Are you praying regularly? Personally? As a family? What can we do to assist you in your prayer life?
- Do you have daily family worship in your home? Can we help you?
- How may we pray for you?
- Are there ways our church may assist you in these areas for which you've asked for prayer?

Other questions will come to mind as you come to understand the members of your congregation and their particular needs.

Christians appreciate sincere concern for their spiritual

well-being. If you listen patiently, most of your members will be grateful for your care.

Don't be surprised if people share material and physical needs with you that have gone unnoticed—large medical bills, pending loss of employment, lack of insurance, and the like. If your church has skilled deacons, you can work to involve them with the family. If your deacons have little experience in the ministry of mercy, then you can help them learn how to care for the spiritual and material needs of your flock.

When someone shares a prayer request with you, *write it down*. Continue to remember the person in your prayers, and follow up in a few days. It's wrong to tell someone you will pray for them and fail to do so. It's uncaring not to stay in touch. After all, the person has summoned the courage to share a burden. Keep close to the family as they struggle.

How to Conclude a Visit

When it is time to end the visit, I do three things.

First, I share a brief Bible passage. For example, I might read Psalm 119:105 and note that in a dark world the Bible functions as a light that shows us the direction in which we need to walk and where the obstacles are that would trip us up.

Then I might quote from memory Westminster Shorter Catechism 90: "That the Word may become effectual to salvation, we must attend thereunto with diligence, preparation, and prayer; receive it with faith and love, lay it up in our hearts, and practice it in our lives." Then I note that God's Word functions as a lamp for our feet and a light for our path:

- As we receive it with faith and love (believing it to be God's Word to us).

- As we lay it up in our hearts (through meditation and memorization).
- As we practice it in our lives (doing what it commands).

Next, I pray, asking God to help us to live according to his Word, and also praying for the special prayer requests that have been made during the visit and for the broader needs of our church. We pray not only because God answers prayer, but also because many people do not have the blessing of hearing other people pray aloud specifically for them. Your prayers will be deeply appreciated.

Finally, I leave a book, booklet, or tract that I believe will encourage the person or family. After you have left the home, the work that you have begun can continue through solid, Bible-centered reading materials. Shedd wisely notes:

> The studious, thoughtful Christian is always more unworldly and sincere, than the Christian who reads but little and thinks still less. The pastor can employ no means more certain to sanctify his flock, than reading and reflection, upon their part. Just in proportion as he is able to induce the habit of studying the Scriptures, and of perusing doctrinal and religious books, will he spiritualize the church to which he ministers.[4]

Involving Your Elders

An effective way to multiply your ministry of visitation is to take an elder with you when you visit. He will learn by your example (or, in some cases, you by his), and when he is confident enough, he will be able to make visits without you.

Here are some "what ifs" that elders might ask:

4. Shedd, *Homiletics and Pastoral Theology*, 326.

What if someone has a complaint about the pastor or a church program?

Ask for permission to go to the pastor or person responsible and tell him about the problem. Then he can speak with the person you are visiting and seek to resolve the matter. These are opportunities, not for conflict, but for growth in mutual understanding and unity in Christ.

What if someone is sick?

Remind the person that, on the basis of James 5:14–15, the elders would count it a privilege to come and pray for him.

What if someone brings up a problem that needs immediate attention, but I am unqualified to help with it?

Encourage the elder to pass along that invitation to you, and you can find appropriate help.

If I am a man, will I ever be asked to visit a single woman?

No, an elder should not visit a single woman by himself. When elders visit the home of a single woman, they should do so in pairs. Integrity and propriety must be hallmarks of every area of church life, including the visitation program. Similarly, a man and a woman should not visit a home together unless they are married.

In churches where elder visits build on an existing relationship of trust between the elders and the female member, this visit should not be awkward.

At other times, and especially if a single woman is new to the church, this kind of visit can be intimidating and uncomfortable. More than discomfort can be at stake. Elders must always be sensitive to women who have experienced abusive personal and church relationships.

When a single woman visits our congregation, I may visit

her with my wife, but we prefer to invite her to our home. Through the years, we have made a place at our dinner table for single women who have become a part of our family's life. After a trusting relationship develops, the routine shepherding care of elders is seen as it should be—one of the privileges of membership in Christ's church.

When Home Visitation Is Not Possible

Several factors make home visitation difficult.

First, there's your schedule. As your congregation grows, making even an annual visit to each home in your congregation can prove difficult. And then there are your members' schedules. Many families are overbooked and reluctant to put you on their calendars.

Finally, some members may not want a home visit. Children are being put to bed. Visits may be considered unwelcome intrusions into their privacy. Respect the wishes of these families. As time goes by and their confidence in you increases, this may change.

Honestly, I must confess that during my three decades in ministry, regular home visitation has become increasingly difficult. So I have developed work-arounds. They are not ideal, but have proved profitable. When home visits are not possible:

- Use the telephone. People will become accustomed to your checking in with them. Some people appreciate scheduling phone calls in advance by email. Whenever you call, begin the phone call with something like this: "Bob, is this a convenient time to talk for ten minutes?" If it's not, ask when would be a more convenient time.
- At the end of a phone conversation, pray. At first, prayer

over the phone might be awkward. Over time, however, people will come to expect it.

- Meet with men or couples in your office or at restaurants. My elders permit me to hire babysitters for the couple when needed.

Before you take your first church, communicate to the pulpit search committee and the church's elders the important place home visitation will take in your ministry. Your pastoral concern and presence will build mutual goodwill and affection, and you will be immeasurably better prepared to intercede for the flock that God has entrusted to your care.

"We are conquerors of the problems that we face only by faith. And Christian hospitality and the community that develops from it is, I believe, the ground zero of our life in Christ: it is how our faith is visible and serviceable, powerful and potent. Hospitality from the home, in the neighborhood, and through the membership of the local congregation has the potential to transform us. Hospitality is our 'by faith' bridge to each other, through Christ."

—ROSARIA CHAMPAGNE BUTTERFIELD[12]

"Contribute to the needs of the saints and seek to show hospitality."

—ROMANS 12:13

"Welcome one another as Christ has welcomed you, for the glory of God."

—ROMANS 15:7

"So then you are no longer strangers and aliens, but you are fellow citizens with the saints and members of the household of God."

—EPHESIANS 2:19

"So, being affectionately desirous of you, we were ready to share with you not only the gospel of God but also our own selves, because you had become very dear to us."

—1 THESSALONIANS 2:8

"Do not neglect to show hospitality to strangers, for thereby some have entertained angels unawares."

—HEBREWS 13:2

"Show hospitality to one another without grumbling."

—1 PETER 4:9

10

Practicing Hospitality[1]

OBJECTIVE: To think creatively about how to make your church and your home places of caring for Christians and non-Christians.

HOSPITALITY OPENS HOMES and hearts to gospel ministry, and will prove an invaluable resource during your first year of ministry.

Let me give my own definition of hospitality: "any direct and personal act of welcoming love, care, or provision given by one Christian to guests or strangers, whether Christian or not." Hospitality is not charity. Charity is most often indirect care, offered through intermediaries, to those in distress. Hospitality is direct and may be offered to anyone, affluent or poor. Ask yourself: "When others come through the door of my church or home, do they understand how much joy it gives me to see them and spend time with them?" I want to make sure I communicate—by my facial expressions, body language, and speech—that they are loved and wanted.

---

1. This chapter appeared in its initial form as a guest column in the *Jackson* (Mississippi) *Clarion-Ledger*, February 26, 2016.

Hospitality Is a Matter of Life and Death

In the ancient world, travel was risky. Inns were notorious for vice and as gathering places for criminals. Christian hospitality opened homes to traveling preachers and merchants, providing places of refuge that assisted the cultivation of Christian friendships and the spread of the gospel.

Cities were frightening places, filled with violence, disease, and danger. Christian hospitality offered newcomers indispensable networks of caring relationships that eased their transition to urban life. To be alone in the city was perilous.

Hospitality was a matter of life and death then. But what about today? In the context of the gospel, hospitality is still a matter of life and death.

Apart from Christ, we were strangers and aliens. But in our Savior, God has welcomed us to his household (Eph. 2:19). Think of those who played a role in your conversion. Perhaps when you were an unbeliever, someone cared for you, and his friendship brought you under the influence of the gospel. For you, hospitality was a matter of spiritual life and death.

An anxious Paul arrived in Corinth, and that city's violence, moral decadence, and idolatry were dreadful. The Lord spoke to him: "Do not be afraid, but go on speaking and do not be silent, for I am with you, and no one will attack you to harm you, for I have many in this city who are my people" (Acts 18:9–10). God's people were in Corinth, but they had not yet heard the gospel of salvation and believed. Paul had to persevere and preach the gospel to them, and then watch the Lord gather them to himself and into his church.

Wherever you minister, there are God's people who at the moment are lost, but are waiting to hear the gospel from you. By welcoming them into your heart and home, you provide a place to proclaim the gospel.

Hospitality Is a Critical Need for Those Barely Hanging On in Your Church

One church lost many members over several years. Some moved away for employment. Others remained in the area, but chose another congregation. The church's leaders conducted a survey to find out why folks left, happy or unhappy.

Members who left satisfied said it was a caring congregation. Members who left the church dissatisfied claimed it was *not* a caring congregation. How can one church be both caring and not caring?

Persons who identified the congregation as caring had experienced brief illnesses, deaths, births, and celebrations, and found the church right there with them.

Persons who judged the church uncaring struggled with chronic illness, depression, doubts about the Christian faith, persistent marriage problems, and rebellious children. Over time, the church's concern for them had waned. The church shouldn't be judged harshly. Haven't you felt powerless to help people and chose to distance yourself, rather than serve men and women in intractable situations? Still, how many would have stayed if they had been recipients of the church's care?

I have been asked for the solution to this critical problem in the church: How do you stick with people in your church who don't seem to find the relief they need? How do you persevere with church members and their enduring problems?

The place to begin is with this core commitment: God's minister does not give up on his people. Has your Savior given up on you? Persevere with people. Hear their frustrations. Sympathize with their hurts. Then talk to your church leaders or other ministers about those people and their trials. Solutions not obvious to you may be clear to them.

Sometimes it will become apparent that another church

may provide more effective care. Don't be afraid to discuss that possibility. For example, I have known some churches that are especially skilled in ministering to people after divorce. If, for whatever reason, your congregation will not care for a divorced person, help that person locate a faithful congregation that will.

Hospitality is also a matter of critical importance to you, the minister. *You must learn to receive the church's care.*

I was slow to recognize this. Although I would never have articulated this point or advised ministers to act in this way, for years I kept my congregations' leaders at a distance. I was there to serve them, I thought, not the other way around.

But at a point when I was struggling with my health and particularly stressful ministry issues, I went to my elders and asked for a pastoral care committee that would meet with Lynne and me to listen, counsel, encourage, and pray. Three elders and their wives hosted us in their homes quarterly, and we were able to share openly and honestly. When health returned, we kept right on meeting. Now I couldn't imagine my ministry without the support of this kind of group.

This leads me to a critical point about hospitality: hospitality requires grace on the part of the one who extends hospitality, and it requires grace on the part of the one who receives it. One of the most difficult life lessons for me to learn has been to receive kindness from others—kindness I need!

What Does Hospitality Look Like?

Hospitality might mean:

- Welcoming visitors to your worship service.
- Hosting a dinner or preparing a meal.
- Extending the hand of friendship to someone who needs your help.

- Helping people move into their new home.
- Cleaning someone's house.
- Opening your home to allow someone to die, surrounded by people who love him.
- Making room at your dinner table for those without family in town.

You want to create a culture of responsiveness in your church. When there's a need, the church responds quickly. When there is a newcomer to your community, your church must embrace him swiftly.

Early in our marriage, Lynne and I decided we would take every opportunity for hospitality given to us. When we take an opportunity to be hospitable, we are offering our friendship, whether it is with a Christian or not.

Practical Tips

- Agree with your spouse (if you are married). How frequently you host and the shape your hospitality takes must be determined together. You can't impose your vision for hospitality upon your wife.
- Hosting does not have to be expensive. Share a cup of coffee, or host a dessert. Hosting is *not* entertaining. Entertaining someone is designed to impress; hospitality is designed to welcome, befriend, comfort, and care.
- For those who do host meals, expenses add up. Two of our congregations added our hosting costs to the church's budget; we were reimbursed for our expenses. Talk with your elders, so they may see the benefits to the church.
- Include your guests in setup and cleanup. This may be awkward at first, but it builds camaraderie, friendship, and teamwork, and makes regular hospitality manageable.

A verse that means much to me is 1 Thessalonians 2:8: "So, being affectionately desirous of you, we were ready to share with you not only the gospel of God but also our own selves, because you had become very dear to us." There you have the basics of hospitality, of Christian ministry: share the gospel; share yourself; treat people with tender affection.

"I, Paul, myself entreat you, by the meekness and gentleness of Christ."
—2 CORINTHIANS 10:1

"Therefore, having put away falsehood, let each one of you speak the truth with his neighbor, for we are members one of another."
—EPHESIANS 4:25

"Him we proclaim, warning everyone and teaching everyone with all wisdom, that we may present everyone mature in Christ. For this I toil, struggling with all his energy that he powerfully works within me."
—COLOSSIANS 1:28–29

"Let the word of Christ dwell in you richly, teaching and admonishing one another in all wisdom, singing psalms and hymns and spiritual songs, with thankfulness in your hearts to God."
—COLOSSIANS 3:16

"But exhort one another every day, as long as it is called 'today,' that none of you may be hardened by the deceitfulness of sin."
—HEBREWS 3:13

11

Counseling

OBJECTIVE: To know when you should counsel church members and when you should refer them to another qualified caregiver.

APPROACH COUNSELING WITH caution and confidence during your first years of ministry.

Be Cautious and Recognize Your Limitations

Few pastors are competent to counsel their members about every issue they face, and that is especially true at the start of one's ministry. Know your limitations. Before the need arises, find counselors who will be available to help.

Identifying people who can help you in no way diminishes your readiness for pastoral ministry. You should firmly believe that the Word of God is sufficient to direct your congregation in the life that pleases God.

The Word is sufficient, but no minister's grasp of it is comprehensive, and neither is his understanding of his members exhaustive. The wise pastor seeks to make available all the godly resources that lie beyond his own local church.

In many cases, counseling persons with histories of substance abuse, addictive behaviors, trauma, mental illness, and psychotropic prescriptions must include the involvement of professional counselors and physicians. Referral becomes an abdication of pastoral responsibility only when a Christian is sent to an ungodly or unskilled counselor. So before you refer, do your homework.

When you recommend a godly and competent counselor to a suffering parishioner, the counselor becomes your partner in caring—augmenting your pastoral care with his skilled direction. Remember, you remain the pastor of the member you refer. You still pursue his holiness in Christ. A good referral takes advantage of the wisdom and expertise of the broader Christian church and puts it to work on behalf of your congregation.

Right now you are lacking experience and skills, and this imposes limits on the scope of care you are able to offer. Time is another reason you may need to refer. Even if you bring strong counseling skills to the pastorate, you still need working relationships with counselors. You cannot be intensely involved with the personal issues of each member of a growing congregation. The needs are too great. And here's the really sad thing: the more gifted you are at counseling, the more people will seek your counsel. If you're not careful, the time you need to prepare for sermons and teaching, to deliver routine pastoral care, and to oversee church administration will disappear. Sadly, your success as a counselor can contribute to your failing in the shepherding work to which God has called you.

But most of us, at the start of our ministries, are not skilled counselors. It takes time and experience to develop, which is why working relationships with counselors are so important. You can be quickly pushed beyond the limits of your ability— and so can your congregation. As the moral dissolution of our society accelerates at a frightening pace, even mature congregations can be overwhelmed by the counseling needs of their members. They lack the personal resources and the practical know-how to adequately care for the long-term consequences of addictive behaviors, trauma, and broken family systems that transmit irresponsible conduct from generation to generation.

A good counselor can help you incorporate the counselee into the larger body of Christ. He or she deals specifically with the deep ravages of sin, and those who have experience address these most capably.

Wise professional counselors also recognize common patterns of behavior and biblical prescriptions for needed change. Their experience gives them an understanding of what repentance looks like and the direction that the walk of faith must take.

I am an experienced pastor and do a fair amount of counseling. Still, I need help. Several years ago, I went to talk with a colleague in our seminary's counseling program. I needed advice on a kind of sinful behavior that I had never seen. I had never seen it, but my colleague had—and, sadly, plenty of times. The fruit of his many years of experience and research helped me to counsel wisely. You will need that kind of resource in your first church.

Approach counseling with caution, and recognize your limits.

Counsel with Confidence

I have advised caution. Nevertheless, you must counsel with confidence. You are God's shepherd to encourage, guide, admonish, and protect your sheep. Here are key elements to keep in mind as you approach counseling in ministry.

Pray

Remember the people you counsel and bring them before the throne of grace. The Lord alone opens hearts and minds. He revives hope in the despairing, consoles the crushed in spirit, reclaims the erring, and gives strength to establish disciplined and righteous habits. In your private prayers, intercede for those who receive your counsel. And pray aloud with them. As you do, you teach them how to articulate their heart concerns to God and appeal to his aid.

Define Counseling Broadly

Don't think of counseling as an activity confined to the pastor's study when people seek out your help to deal with specific sins and problems. That's only a small part of counseling.

Every time you preach, you open up the Word that reproves, corrects, and trains in righteousness (2 Tim. 3:16). You proclaim the Word of the risen and reigning Christ, who has made provision for the sanctification of his people. Biblical preaching forms the character that leads people away from the sins that defile the conscience and disrupt relationships.

Biblical teaching, whether from the pulpit or in a counseling session, instructs in righteousness and helps parishioners lay aside ungodly habits and develop godly ones. By admonishing and teaching, you strive to present men and women mature to the Savior (Col. 1:28–29).

Be a Student

Read pastoral counseling books and journal articles. Spend time with seasoned pastoral counselors. Take online courses; abundant resources are available.

Opportunities for Counseling Are Many

Early in my ministry, there was little in the way of financial counseling resources. I discovered that I had some ability to help folks establish a budget and keep it, and to develop strategies for paying off debt. Before the days of personal computers, I typed résumés for members, and then began to do interview coaching and, when possible, shop the résumés in my network of businessmen.

Budgets and résumé preparation may sound far removed from pastoral ministry and counseling, but they are not. Financial discipline and finding a job are integral to providing income for family and church. Time focused on these areas led inevitably to conversations about the life of faith, dependence on the Lord, godly disciplines, unity in the home, and numerous other issues.

Listen Patiently

When someone seeks your counsel, don't hurry to offer advice. Solomon counsels: "If one gives an answer before he hears, it is his folly and shame" (Prov. 18:13). Resist the impulse to offer quick solutions. If you speak into situations you don't understand, it builds ill will and causes people to lose confidence in you. People will come to you with problems and sins that they may have struggled with for years. Do you really think you can offer a solution in a matter of minutes? In order to care for the person in front of you, you must listen to him for understanding and not listen for the purpose of responding.

Be Fair

"The one who states his case first seems right, until the other comes and examines him" (Prov. 18:17). Whether the problem is a strained marriage or two church members in conflict, it's beneficial, when possible, to listen to the concerns of all parties involved. You must realize that some people come to the pastor, not for guidance, but to find support for their side of an argument. Blinded by anger or ignorant of their own motivations, they want to win an argument or force change upon their adversary. This need to be right is more important to them than the glory of God and their own personal sanctification.

Receive Personal Counsel

One of the by-products of receiving mature counsel is that your counselor also becomes a role model. Don't wait until problems become crises. Benefit from wise pastors and professional counselors who will not only promote your growth in Christ, but also show you how the work is done.

When Lynne and I were considering seeking another pastoral call, we went to a professional counselor who was well known for getting couples to ask the right questions and make decisions based on mutual understanding. We were not in conflict. We only wanted to decide wisely. Our counselor not only gave us a clear direction, but also gave me a model for counseling that I have since found very helpful.

Some Situations Are Impervious to Change

Just as some health problems are intractable, so, too, will many relational problems—a gospel-hardened spouse, a wayward child, and chronic depression, to name a few—prove intractable over time. This does not mean that we stop praying for a change of circumstances, but prayers become much more focused on honoring the Lord in adversity and seeking contentment in suffering.

Expect Disappointments

Others will disappoint you. Biblical counsel will be rejected. A couple seems to make tremendous progress, and then one of them walks away from the marriage. Sinful habits that were apparently broken have returned. Counseling that results ultimately in a harvest of righteousness can be marred by numerous and frustrating setbacks.

Expect many disappointments. Be patient, even as the Lord is patient with you. Persevere, for the Lord perseveres with you.

You will disappoint yourself. Inevitably there will be times when your counsel is wrong. You weren't in command of the facts, or the passing of time reveals a better path that was not taken. You gave counsel that, in hindsight and with the benefit of experience and maturity, now seems less than wise. This cannot be helped. Even apart from our own sinfulness, we are finite. Our insights into troubled people and relationships are never perfect.

In times of disappointment, certainty of your ministerial calling and love for people will enable you to continue serving. And most of all, your own personal dealings with "the Father of mercies and God of all comfort" will encourage you. He comforts you and me in afflictions, so that we may comfort the afflicted "with the comfort with which we ourselves are comforted by God" (2 Cor. 1:3–4).

"Therefore a man shall leave his father and mother and hold fast to his wife, and the two shall become one flesh.' This mystery is profound, and I am saying that it refers to Christ and the church. However, let each one of you love his wife as himself, and let the wife see that she respects her husband."

—EPHESIANS 5:31–33

12

Weddings

OBJECTIVE: To build a checklist of what you must do before your first wedding. Officiating at weddings is among ministry's great joys, so be ready for it.

IT IS AN honor to be asked to perform a wedding. You join together in marriage a couple whom you have helped to prepare for a lifetime of service—both to one another and to the Lord.

Many good resources are available for pastors as they prepare couples for marriage. My purpose here is not to provide comprehensive instruction, but to suggest several things to keep in mind as you think about your first wedding and your duties to the couple who look to you for guidance. As joyous as a wedding is, there are pitfalls that can create hardship and pain for you, the couple, and your church. Most of these can be avoided if you think carefully before you are asked to perform your first wedding.

Begin with your new church's wedding policy. Soon after arriving at your first church, determine whether it has a written one. The document should cover basic concerns such as:

- May only members and children of members be married in the church, or is there an application process for those outside the church?

- Is premarital counseling required?
- Who approves applications for marriage? The elders? The minister? The minister and elders?
- What music may be used in a wedding service? Who may play or sing? Who makes the final decision regarding musicians and music?
- Are there restrictions on flash photography?
- What about candles? Can furniture at the front of the sanctuary be rearranged?
- What are the fees for sanctuary use? For musicians? For janitorial services?
- Are the marriage vows prescribed, or is there flexibility?
- Does the church identify who will serve as the wedding coordinator?
- What is the policy for receptions and dinners on church property? May alcoholic beverages be served?

Do not ignore your church's wedding policy. If you plunge ahead with a wedding that does not meet your church's guidelines, you will likely find yourself in controversy that may damage your future effectiveness. If your church does not have a wedding policy, do some research and recommend to your elders a basic set of guidelines. Leaders should be in agreement about who can be married at the church and what is permitted at weddings.

Sadly, because of the rapidly changing legal and moral climate in America, it may be prudent to have an attorney review your church's wedding policy. Of special concern are weddings for those outside the church. Assess the risk of litigation if you were to refuse to rent your facility on moral grounds, an act that may lead to an accusation of discrimination. Because of the possibility of litigation, some churches restrict the use of their building to the weddings of members and their children.

Let's assume that your first church has no wedding policy. Here is my advice *before* a couple comes and asks you to perform your first wedding. Communicate to your elders that you will not perform weddings without their approval for two reasons:

First, you need their wisdom. They may have many years of experience with the couple and be familiar with family dynamics within the congregation. Think through your first wedding with this truth in mind: "Without counsel plans fail, but with many advisers they succeed" (Prov. 15:22). Look to your elders for their advice as you consider all matters related to marriages and weddings.

Second, you need their protection. If you must decline to perform a wedding, then you want to have your elders, if possible, standing behind the decision. For example, suppose a prominent family in the church wants you to officiate at the marriage of their child to an unbeliever. You will want your church officers backing you up when you say no.

Wedding policies take time to develop. So address the fundamental issues with your elders before they are needed. Early in your tenure, seek their approval of three policies:

- The elders must approve all requests for weddings at the church.
- Couples must schedule premarital counseling from you or another qualified person before approval for the wedding is given.
- You will not, under any circumstances, officiate at the wedding of a believer to an unbeliever. At a minimum, this means that both persons must be members in good standing of a biblically faithful church.

Other policies can be written over time, but these are fundamental.

Now let's talk about the couple who want you to be the minister leading their wedding service. How do you begin the conversation?

- Communicate to the couple how happy you are for them and that you are honored to be asked and delighted to be a part of their lives at this special time.
- If you don't know the couple well, ask them to share their story. How did they meet? What led to their decision to marry?
- Explain that your church wants the very best for couples. To achieve that goal, the elders require that a couple complete premarital counseling before you agree to perform their wedding. That counseling can be under your direction or that of another qualified person.
- Also explain that all weddings must meet with your elders' approval.
- In all your conversations, communicate your heartfelt desire that their marriage get off to the best start possible.

What Are the Basics of Premarital Counseling?[1]

A key principle in premarital counseling, one that you want the couple to take to heart, is that *marriage does not solve problems.* If a man is habitually angry before marriage, he'll be so after marriage. A woman is foolish to think that marriage will change his behavior. Likewise, a man deceives himself if he thinks that marriage to him is just the cure for his fiancée's

---

1. If possible, couples should agree to counseling before their engagement, not just before their marriage. Once rings are given, dates are set, and families are committed, the pressure to marry can be overwhelming. A couple in premarital counseling may begin to sense that marriage might be unwise, but feel compelled to go ahead with the wedding to avoid embarrassment. It is far better to make the decision not to proceed *before* the engagement is announced.

chronic discontent. Two financially reckless people will have a financially reckless marriage; count on it.

In counseling, couples will test their abilities to solve problems together. Do differences lead to angry words or withdrawal, or are they able to work toward resolving problems with honest words, patient listening, good questions, and respect? If you are a counselor prone to talk during much of a counseling session, you must restrain yourself. The overtalkative pastor is a poor listener. There will be time for instruction, but the couple need to be talking with each other, and you must learn to ask the questions that prompt and guide their conversation. Discipline yourself to listen attentively. Good ministers are good listeners.

What Ground Should You Cover in Premarital Counseling?

Personal faith. Have both individuals made public profession of faith in Christ? Are they members in good standing of a biblically faithful church? Do they regularly attend church? Do they share the same attitudes toward doctrine, worship, and the sanctification of the Lord's Day? Do they support the worship and work of the church? Do they have a good grasp of and commitment to Christian ethics? As individuals, do they have a devotional life? What are their expectations for family devotions and worship?

Holiness. Each individual must honestly think through these questions: Does our relationship increase my commitment to personal holiness? Does it strengthen my devotion to the Lord and his church? Is our relationship founded upon a shared commitment to Christian ethics, or have I lowered my standards in order to achieve and maintain a relationship with this person?

Family histories. Do both sets of parents approve of the marriage? What was it like to grow up in their homes? How did their families celebrate birthdays and holidays, and how do they recognize personal achievements? What ways of handling problems did they learn from their parents? How does the prospective husband treat his mother? The son who acts contemptuously toward his mother will almost certainly continue that behavior with his wife.

Personal histories. These include difficult questions: Have they been married before? Have all physical and mental health issues been disclosed and discussed? Have past relationships and sexual histories been discussed? Are there children from a previous marriage or other relationship, and what are the expectations for the parent and stepparent in the new marriage?

Wedding vows. Review the wedding vows. In this context, you can present the biblical foundations of marriage. Do the couple understand and agree with the biblical foundations of marriage?

Finances. How do the couple view money? Has all debt been disclosed? Do they have a personal budget? Have they discussed a family budget? Do they share a similar outlook on money and its uses, including contributing to the church? Do they need to attend a financial seminar or meet with a mature Christian who can provide sound financial counsel?

Work. What is their attitude toward work? I have seen hardworking women marry "boys" who expend enormous amounts of their time playing video games and watching sports, rather than working hard at their jobs, earning a good and steady income, serving the church, helping at home, and spending time with their families. An immature attitude toward work will quickly fill a marriage with sorrow.

Recreation and leisure. In their opinion, what is the ideal way to spend discretionary time?

Sex. What is the couple's attitude and expectation toward sex? Be attentive to concerns about pornography. If the sin is not confessed and repented of before marriage, it will continue in marriage. Remember, *marriage does not solve problems.*

Children. What are their expectations regarding the number of children, how they will raise them, and their participation in the life of the church?

You must be a good listener. Observe how the couple discuss issues. Do they avoid difficult subjects? Are there indications that they do not respect each other? When dealing with a personal problem, do they accuse each other or blame their problems on someone else? Does either of them avoid taking responsibility for bad behavior or decisions?

Ministerial Protocol

As a new minister, you will receive invitations from family and friends in other congregations to do their weddings. You should never consent to participate without the approval of the minister of the congregation where the wedding will be performed. He is the shepherd of that flock, and laboring in his field is by his invitation only.

I was thrilled when one of our sons and his fiancée asked me to officiate at their wedding. But my reply was, "I'd be delighted, *if* your pastor requests that I assist him." Happily, he did, and we shared in leading the service together. Never perform any ministerial duty in another congregation without the invitation of that congregation's minister.

Conclusion

Jesus' first miracle was performed at the wedding at Cana of Galilee. Our Savior gathered with a couple and their families to feast and rejoice. Many festive occasions will come your way as you lead services of Christian marriage. The good foundations you have laid in premarital counseling will make these times even more joyous. Truly, it is an honor to be asked to perform a wedding!

"The Lord Jesus makes no mistakes in managing his friends' affairs. He orders all their concerns with perfect wisdom: all things happen at the right time, and in the right way. He gives them as much of sickness and as much of health, as much of poverty and as much of riches, as much of sorrow and as much of joy, as he sees their souls require. He leads them by the right way to bring them to the city of habitation. He mixes their bitterest cups like a wise physician, and takes care that they have not a drop too little or too much. His people often misunderstand his dealings; they are silly enough to fancy their course of life might have been better ordered: but in the resurrection day they will thank God that not their will, but Christ's, was done."

—J. C. RYLE[13]

"And Jesus went throughout all the cities and villages, teaching in their synagogues and proclaiming the gospel of the kingdom and healing every disease and every affliction. When he saw the crowds, he had compassion for them, because they were harassed and helpless, like sheep without a shepherd."

—MATTHEW 9:35–36

"Blessed be the God and Father of our Lord Jesus Christ, the Father of mercies and God of all comfort, who comforts us in all our affliction, so that we may be able to comfort those who are in any affliction, with the comfort with which we ourselves are comforted by God."

—2 CORINTHIANS 1:3–4

"Is anyone among you sick? Let him call for the elders of the church, and let them pray over him, anointing him with oil in the name of the Lord."

—JAMES 5:14

13

Hospital and Hospice Care

OBJECTIVE: To cultivate a love for being with sick and dying people in their time of great need.

You WILL SPEND countless hours among the sick. This time will be precious to you. You minister in the name of the Savior, who welcomed the sick who were brought to him. Now he sends you to the sick to pray, comfort, and minister his Word. And because you love your flock, you will want to be with them.[1]

While you care for the sick, your emotions will rise and fall like a roller coaster. In one waiting room, you lead the family in thanksgiving for successful surgery; in another, you seek God's sustaining grace—the tumor is inoperable.

On the same day, you visit one wing of a hospital to celebrate a child's birth and then move to another wing to sit with a patient receiving his chemo treatments: happiness in one room, painful perseverance and uncertainty in the other. At one bedside, a patient honestly confesses his fears; at another, the dying believer confesses his faith with such rock-solid

---

1. For excellent counsel on visiting the sick, see Brian Croft, *Visit the Sick: Ministering God's Grace in Times of Illness* (Grand Rapids: Zondervan, 2014).

confidence that you leave the room inspired, your own faith strengthened.

Almost certainly, you will be anxious on your first trips to the hospital. The steps you should take, the words you should speak, and the prayers you should offer are not immediately clear. That's to be expected. Your understanding of how best to care for the sick will grow as you obtain experience, for experience is an indispensable teacher.

Gathering experience takes time. So right now pay attention to a few things to help you keep your poise:

Watch

Before you accept your first pastoral call, study your pastoral mentors and ask to be included in their hospital visits. Three of my ministers included me in many hospital visits before I became a student pastor. Their ministries to the sick became clinics in pastoral care.

Go

When notified that a member of your congregation has been unexpectedly rushed to the hospital, go. Don't wait. If the situation is critical, you want to be with the family as soon as possible. Christians expect their pastor to be with them in crises like this—don't disappoint or keep them waiting.

When You Arrive

Introduce yourself if you don't know all the family members. Someone may have called you and filled in the details. If not, or if details are sketchy, gently inquire. "I heard that Bob is here, and I came as soon as I could. Please tell me his situation." Even if they have little information to communicate, pray with the family. Assure them of the church's prayers.

While the family waits for information, sit with them in the waiting room. Don't worry about what to say. Young ministers may feel a need to say something to break the silence. Resist the impulse. Just sit. When a family member talks, listen carefully. Speak when appropriate. Be ready to get water or tissues.

If the patient is alert, the family will probably want you to see him in the ER. Keep your visit brief. Conclude with an appropriate Bible passage and pray.

What if the doctor informs the family that their loved one is dead, or offers little or no hope of recovery? The shock will be severe, especially if it is unexpected. Keep in mind that although you weep with those who weep, you must always be in control of your emotions. (This does not mean that you may not shed a tear!) In times of great sadness, communicate your sympathy with the grieving—you will grieve, too. Hug them. Assure them that you love them. But by word and tone of voice, convey trust in God, who is both our Sovereign King and ever-loving heavenly Father. His power never wanes; his love never falters; his devotion to his adopted children endures forever.

Routine Hospital Visits

When to Visit

Ordinarily, you will want to visit during visiting hours. At some hospitals, there are better times to visit than others—hours when doctors' rounds, testing, and physical therapy are predictable. Inquire at the hospital. Ask a local minister what the best time is to visit. Besides obtaining useful information, you will be looking to other local clergy as partners in ministry.

At certain times during the day, the traffic becomes gridlocked at large hospitals, especially during shift changes and rush hour. Your time is valuable, and you will want to avoid the hospital at those times.

Conducting the Visit

Knock. Before you enter the room, knock and identify yourself. That gives the patient time to adjust her clothes or bedcovers. She may ask you to wait a moment. Never be in a rush.

At the bedside, communicate how glad you are to see the patient. If the patient says that she knows you're busy and hopes that she hasn't inconvenienced you, don't tell her that you're just doing your job. That's the wrong response! You are there because you love and care for her, and are concerned about her physical and spiritual welfare.

She will likely share updates. Listen. How are her spirits? Is she frightened? Anxious? Confident in the Lord? All of the above?

Don't camp out. Routine hospital visits should be brief. Why? First of all, a hospital is a place for treatment and recovery. Long visits are unhelpfully exhausting. Don't work against the health interests of the patient.

Doctors, nurses, therapists, and nutritionists make their rounds. Stay out of their way. Other family and friends drop by, and if the patient is receiving visitors, you must not keep them away. Interruptions are a fact of life in a hospital. So avoid pointless conversation and don't stay long.

How long? My visits are seldom more than ten or fifteen minutes, and frequently shorter. Since 1983, the Rev. Brister Ware has served as minister of pastoral care at First Presbyterian

Church in Jackson, Mississippi. He recommends standing by the bedside with your weight on one leg. When you feel the need to shift to the other leg, it's time to leave.

At rehab facilities and with patients under hospice care, my visits are longer and have more of the feel of a home visit. The days are long, the pace is less hectic, and patients welcome time with you.

Inside voice, please. The hospital is not the place for boisterous talk and laughter. A loud voice jars. Instead of jarring, soothe. Speak loud enough to be understood, but no louder.

It's not about you. As the patient talks about his situation, you might recall times when you were sick and faced a similar experience. You might even feel the urge to tell a story—but don't. Time is precious. The patient does not need to concentrate on your life story. Nor should you shift attention away from the sick. Keep your focus on the person in the bed.

Before You Leave

Read Scripture. I find it helpful to think ahead of time what passage to share. Apart from Psalms, I read most frequently from 2 Corinthians. As you read through the Bible, mark down passages that would be helpful when visiting the sick. Read your Bible as a pastor who must skillfully bring its truths to needy people in a variety of circumstances.

Has the Lord granted recovery? Psalm 40:1–5. Will the path forward be long, difficult, and painful? Romans 5:1–5. Is the patient's health declining and irreversible? 2 Corinthians 4:16–5:10. Has the patient confessed a sin? Psalm 32, Psalm 51, or Romans 5:6–11. Is he concerned about his Christian witness to friends and family? 2 Corinthians 1:3–7 or 4:7–12. Is she uncertain about her ability to meet the challenges ahead? Psalm 23, 2 Corinthians 12:1–10, or 1 Peter 1:3–9. Does she need fresh assurance of the hope of heaven? Revelation 21:1–7.

Pray. Work the passage of Scripture into your prayer. For example, if you have read Psalm 32, pray that the patient will experience the joy of sins forgiven. You've been listening carefully; now work the patient's concerns into your prayer. Always, always communicate the comfort of the gospel—that we rest secure in the love of a Savior who lived a perfect life for us and died a substitutionary death for our sins.

What about prayers for healing? We pray for the restoration of health for the sick. But we also know that God, for his own glory and the good of his people, frequently says no (Rom. 8:26–39; 2 Cor. 12:1–10). So we also pray for God's sustaining grace, which proves sufficient in every trial. And finally, he can answer the prayer for healing by calling the believer home to heaven, safe from the reach of sickness, pain, and sorrow. The catechism offers consolation to God's grieving people as it summarizes gospel truth: "The souls of believers are at their death made perfect in holiness, and do immediately pass into glory; and their bodies, being still united to Christ, do rest in their graves till the resurrection."[2]

Visiting the Dying

Hospice care enables loved ones to die at home, surrounded by family and friends. In many cases, the months at home provide you with extended time with the believer.

Things to Discuss with the Dying

The gospel. Over and over again, return to the assurances of the gospel. The Heidelberg Catechism asks, "What is your only comfort in life and death?" Eloquently and movingly it answers: "That I am not my own, but belong—body and soul,

---

2. Westminster Shorter Catechism 37.

in life and in death—to my faithful Savior Jesus Christ. He has fully paid for all my sins with his precious blood, and has set me free from the tyranny of the devil. He also watches over me in such a way that not a hair can fall from my head without the will of my Father in heaven: in fact, all things must work together for my salvation. Because I belong to him, Christ, by his Holy Spirit, assures me of eternal life and makes me whole-heartedly willing and ready from now on to live for him."[3]

End-of-life issues. Are there end-of-life issues to be discussed with the dying or his family? These include accepting and refusing treatment.[4]

Relationships. Are there broken relationships that need restoration? Does the dying believer need to confess wrongs and ask for forgiveness? Do you need to encourage another family member to confess sins against the dying person and to seek her forgiveness?

Will. Has a will been prepared? Is it current? If the dying person expresses his desire for the disposition of his assets, then ask whether he has made this clear in his will.

The salvation of family members. Are there unbelieving family members who weigh on her heart? Will you have the opportunity to speak to them?

At the Deathbed

When a family calls and informs you that death is imminent, go to the home or hospital. Even if it means staying up

3. Heidelberg Catechism 1, https://www.urcna.org/1651/file_retrieve/23908 (accessed September 18, 2017).

4. Good resources for end-of-life issues include John Jefferson Davis, *Evangelical Ethics: Issues Facing the Church Today* (Phillipsburg, NJ: P&R Publishing, 2016); David VanDrunen, *Bioethics and the Christian Life: A Guide to Making Difficult Decisions* (Wheaton, IL: Crossway, 2009); Gilbert Meilaender, *Bioethics: A Primer for Christians* (Grand Rapids: Eerdmans, 2005); Bill Davis, *Departing in Peace: Biblical Decision-Making at the End of Life* (Phillipsburg, NJ: P&R Publishing, 2017).

all night, stay with the dying. During that time, read Scripture and pray with the family. Some families sing hymns at the bedside of the dying. Sing with them. Even if the believer has been unconscious for days, assume that he hears everything. Let him hear the words and songs of faith! The victorious death is the death of one who dies in faith surrounded by people of faith.

Conclusion

God has called you to be with the sick. As you go, God will use the ministry of his Word to strengthen and comfort them. Time and time again, your own faith will be strengthened as you see God's work in the lives of his afflicted and beloved people.

"It is better to go to the house of mourning than to go to the house of feasting, for this is the end of all mankind, and the living will lay it to heart."

—ECCLESIASTES 7:2

"Weep with those who weep."

—ROMANS 12:15

"Yes, we are of good courage, and we would rather be away from the body and at home with the Lord."

—2 CORINTHIANS 5:8

"For to me to live is Christ, and to die is gain."

—PHILIPPIANS 1:21

"But we do not want you to be uninformed, brothers, about those who are asleep, that you may not grieve as others do who have no hope. For since we believe that Jesus died and rose again, even so, through Jesus, God will bring with him those who have fallen asleep. For this we declare to you by a word from the Lord, that we who are alive, who are left until the coming of the Lord, will not precede those who have fallen asleep. For the Lord himself will descend from heaven with a cry of command, with the voice of an archangel, and with the sound of the trumpet of God. And the dead in Christ will rise first. Then we who are alive, who are left, will be caught up together with them in the clouds to meet the Lord in the air, and so we will always be with the Lord. Therefore encourage one another with these words."

—1 THESSALONIANS 4:13–18

14

Funerals

OBJECTIVE: To take the right steps to ensure good pastoral care, from news of a person's death to the funeral to long-term care for the bereaved.

CHRISTIANITY IS A religion of resurrection. All life ends in death. Resurrection proclaims that death ends in life. That's good news for a dying world!

When Christians assemble for worship, they unite their voices in proclaiming the One who is the resurrection and the life. Whether gathered at Lord's Day services or for the funerals of precious believers, Christians publicly testify to God's promise of the resurrection of the body and the life everlasting.

At funerals you, Christ's minister, bring comfort. You assure mourners that the soul of the believer, united to Christ, is gone to be with the Lord.

At funerals you, Christ's minister, give hope. You declare that the body rests in the grave, waiting for that great day of resurrection, when the bodies and souls of believers will be reunited, and enter into the new heaven and new earth.

From the time of death until the graveside committal service, *you must not forget the importance of the body*—the lifeless body in the casket and the resurrection body that awaits the deceased. All our longings will be fulfilled when Christ returns in glory. Completely renewed in body and in soul, we will dwell in the house of the Lord forever. Christian funerals proclaim resurrection hope.

You want your congregation to leave the graveside strengthened in faith, hope, and love. But that outcome depends in large part on how you, the pastor, prepare people for death and how you minister the gospel to grieving men and women.

What follows are the duties you must fulfill as you care for your hurting flock.

Prepare Your Congregation

Prepare your people to live holy lives. Prepare them to die trusting in the Lord. That means giving clear teaching about death and dying. Your teaching will not lessen the pain that follows the death of a loved one, but it will prepare your congregation to trust God's sovereign kingship and fatherly care in affliction and bereavement.

What Should Your Teaching Include?

Teach about the origin of death. Death is the terrible wage that sin pays and the just punishment it deserves—both physical death in this life and spiritual death now and in the life to come.

Your congregation should never be surprised by the reality of physical death, nor by what leads up to it—disease, accidents, natural disasters, and physical and mental decline. These are expected in a world under God's judgment. Without the backdrop of divine justice, your congregation is ignorant of the meaning of death. If they are confused about God's wrath against sin, then they will not know how to love the Savior who bore God's wrath in their stead.

Teach about the common curse. There is a suffering that all men and women share, Christian and non-Christian. Cancer strikes unbeliever and believer. Unbelievers die in acts of random violence, and so do Christians. Children of believers and of unbelievers are born with birth defects. Both Christians and non-Christians endure injustice, face natural disasters, suffer from depression, and succumb to the ravages of aging. Christians are not exempt from the sorrows that are common to humanity.

Teach your people how to think about death properly—it will be a sanctifying influence. Louis Berkhof writes pastorally:

> The very thought of death, bereavements through death, the feeling that sicknesses and sufferings are harbingers of death, and the consciousness of the approach of death,— all have a very beneficial effect on the people of God. They serve to humble the proud, to mortify carnality, to check worldliness and to foster spiritual-mindedness. In the mystical union with their Lord believers are made to share the experiences of Christ. Just as He entered upon His glory by the pathway of sufferings and death, they too can enter upon their eternal reward only through sanctification. Death is often the supreme test of the strength of the faith that is in them, and frequently calls forth striking manifestations of the consciousness of victory in the very hour of seeming defeat, I Pet. 4:12, 13. It completes the sanctification of the souls of believers, so that they become at once "the spirits of just men made perfect," Heb. 12:23; Rev. 21:27. Death is not the end for believers, but the beginning of a perfect life.[1]

1. Louis Berkhof, *Systematic Theology* (Grand Rapids: Eerdmans, 1979), 670–71.

The fact of our future death should cultivate seriousness about life, making personal holiness a preeminent concern for both you and your flock. Funerals impress upon believers the urgency of walking in close communion with God. Our forgetfulness of our own mortality is one of the reasons behind Solomon's admonition: "It is better to go to the house of mourning than to go to the house of feasting, for this is the end of all mankind, and the living will lay it to heart" (Eccl. 7:2).

Teach your people about the final judgment that follows death. "It is appointed for man to die once, and after that comes judgment" (Heb. 9:27). There are only two destinations after death, heaven and hell. There are no "do-overs" or second chances.

Teach your people about the intermediate state and the resurrection of the body. Unfold to your congregation the comfort of the intermediate state, the believer's condition between his death and the day of resurrection. To be absent from the body is to be present with the Lord; to live is Christ, and to die is gain (2 Cor. 5:8; Phil. 1:21). In his hour of piercing anguish, Christ comforted a new believer on the threshold of eternity, saying, "Today you will be with me in Paradise" (Luke 23:43). These are the words of comfort that you must earnestly impress upon your congregation.

Talk about the hope of Christ's second coming, when the bodies of believers are raised from the dead and, reunited with their souls, are transformed to be like Christ's glorious body. At the resurrection, they are "made perfectly blessed in the full enjoying of God to all eternity."[2]

Teach your people about the beauty of heaven. Heaven, writes Jonathan Edwards, is a world of perfect love. Unhindered by sin or our fluctuating faith and unstable emotions, we will love God perfectly and experience his love perfectly. In eternal

---

2. Westminster Shorter Catechism 38.

fellowship with each other, believers will be perfectly lovely, perfectly loved, and perfectly loving.[3] Your congregation needs to know that there is for them "an inheritance that is imperishable, undefiled, and unfading, kept in heaven" for them (1 Peter 1:4).

When a family suffers the loss of a loved one, these truths will provide much-needed comfort and strength. But here's what's critical for you to know: you must teach these truths *before* the time of trial. When poorly taught, a grief-stricken person is unable to learn, process, and appropriate the great truths of Scripture. When you gather with a grieving family, it's not the time to correct poor theology. In your preaching, lay the foundation of resurrection hope, so that your congregation may rest upon it in times of sorrow.

I hope that at your first church you find that your predecessors have laid a solid foundation. If not, time must not be wasted. Teach!

In the previous chapter, I discussed ministry to dying people and their families.[4] Now let's consider what you should do after you have been notified of a death in your congregation.[5]

Go

Go to the family to express your love, concern, and sorrow. Quote from memory a passage of Scripture and pray. Sit with the family. If you're new to the congregation, listen to how the family talks about the deceased and about their relationship to him. It will give you some understanding about what shape

3. Jonathan Edwards, *Charity and Its Fruits* (London: Banner of Truth, 1969), 323–68.

4. See chapter 13.

5. For detailed counsel on funerals and care for the grieving, see Warren Wiersbe and David Wiersbe, *Ministering to the Mourning: A Practical Guide for Pastors, Church Leaders, and Other Caregivers* (Chicago: Moody Publishers, 2006).

your pastoral care should take, and it will also provide you with information that you will want to share at the funeral.

Go, even if you will not be part of the funeral. Go, even if the death was expected. Walk with your families in the valley of the shadow of death.

Think about the Family's Needs

Will the family need meals or childcare? Will out-of-town guests or elderly family and friends need transportation from the airport or to the visitation and funeral? Will some of them need places to stay? Are there financial needs? Who in your congregation is available to assist?

Rely on the Funeral Home Director

The funeral home director is the expert. Let him walk the family through routine matters—obituaries, setting the time of the funeral (they'll confirm with you), death certificates, and a host of other issues. When family members ask about these issues, refer them to him.

At the church or funeral home, he will make sure that the pallbearers know what to do, and will line everyone up for the processional. When the service is concluded, he will make sure that everyone leaves the sanctuary in good order.

At the graveside, the funeral director will tell you which end is the head of the casket. He will seat the family, invite others to gather around them, and dismiss the congregation after the service.

Build a good working relationship with the funeral home director(s) in your community. It would be helpful, when you first arrive in town, to find out the funeral home used most frequently by people in your church. As a pastor and new member of the community, ask a funeral director what you need to know about funerals in your community and state.

Plan the Funeral with the Family

After the family has met with the funeral home, gather with them to plan the service. Are there favorite hymns and Scripture readings? Are there stories about the loved one that the family wants you to share? Are there other people they wish to include in the service? In each meeting with the family, read Scripture and pray.

What about Cremation?

More and more Christians choose cremation instead of burial. Reasons vary. But for many, the choice is financial. Cremation is less expensive than a traditional funeral.

Still, my own position is that the whole biblical doctrine of redemption is best represented in a traditional Christian burial. But though I believe a good scriptural case can be made for traditional Christian burial, I do not intend for a moment to cast doubt upon the faith of believers who have chosen cremation. Furthermore, the way in which a body is treated after death does not affect the resurrection of the body.

I make the case for traditional Christian burial in my teaching and writing ministry, and *not* in homes of the grieving. If the family has chosen cremation, I proceed with the family's wishes. No article of the Christian faith is at stake. I advise that you read thoughtful articles on the subject.[6]

6. S. M. Houghton, "Earth to Earth: Considerations on the Practice of Cremation," *Banner of Truth* 70 (July–August 1969): 37–46; David Jones, "To Bury or to Burn? Cremation in Christian Perspective," *The Gospel Coalition*, January 23, 2013, https://www.thegospelcoalition.org/article/to-bury-or-to-burn-cremation-in

Now, here are my reasons for advising burial. That Christ was buried is fundamental to the gospel message (1 Cor. 15:3–4). When buried, Christians follow the path of humiliation taken by their Lord.

The souls of believers, united to Christ, have gone to be with the Lord (2 Cor. 5:8). Yet the body, too, is united to Christ and rests in the grave, awaiting its glorious resurrection (1 Thess. 4:13–18). At the resurrection, the bodies and souls of believers will be reunited, and they will enter into the new heaven and new earth to serve and worship their God. All these truths are beautifully portrayed in a Scripture-based graveside service.

I recommend cherishing the long and rich tradition of Christian burial. At the graveside, Christians publicly proclaim their belief in the resurrection of the body even as they comfort one another in hope.

Know the Essential Parts of a Christian Funeral

Christian funerals should always include Scripture, prayer for comfort and submission to God's will, clear biblical testimony about death, salvation, and the life to come, and the need for everyone to be ready to die.

As you prepare the order of service, obtain bulletins from other funerals at the church. This will give you a sense of your church's customs. Also, your denomination likely has a directory of worship that provides a model order of service for funerals. Other resources are available.[7] Don't act as if you're

---

-christian-perspective (accessed September 29, 2017); John Piper, "Should Christians Cremate Their Loved Ones? A Modest Proposal," April 26, 2016, Desiring God, http://www.desiringgod.org/articles/should-christians-cremate-their-loved -ones (accessed September 29, 2017).

7. For a traditional order of service for funeral and graveside, see Terry L. Johnson, ed., *Leading in Worship*, rev. ed. (White Hall, WV: Tolle Lege Press, 2013).

the first person ever to conduct a funeral. Use the resources available to you.

Know the Goals of a Christian Funeral

As you lead a funeral service, you will strive to:

- Glorify God.
- Honor the Lord Jesus, who is the resurrection and the life.
- Show respect for the human body.
- Remember and give thanks for the life of the deceased.
- Comfort the grieving.
- Point the lost to Jesus.
- Encourage with resurrection hope.

Keep Good Order

As with all Christian gatherings, you should conduct yourself and the funeral service with dignity. That includes keeping good order. At some point in recent decades, it became popular for open microphones to be made available so that mourners could share thoughts about the deceased. On occasion, they give tremendous testimonies to God's grace. But more often there is loss of emotional self-control, venting of frustration, poor theology, and questioning of God's providence. All this is out of keeping with a Christian assembly. We grieve, but not as the world. We grieve with hope and in truth. I strongly discourage open microphones at funerals.

The family may want to have a friend or family member offer remembrances of the deceased, which is perfectly acceptable. If the family entrusts me with this task, I work words of remembrance into the funeral sermon. If a family member would like to share words of remembrance, but is uncertain about controlling his emotions during the service, offer to convey his thoughts for him. He can write them down or you can take notes as he shares thoughts with you in private.

What about the Funeral Sermon?

I always preach a funeral sermon on salvation, death, and resurrection. These sermons are brief, no more than fifteen to twenty minutes in length.

What if the Deceased Was an Unbeliever?

Although we cannot give thanks for the person's faith, we can and should thank the Lord for his life, for his care for family, and for his devotion to community.

I have done funerals for complete scoundrels. In those cases, don't lie about the deceased. Preach the gospel for the comfort of those who do believe and for the conversion of those who don't.

At the Graveside

The graveside service should be brief, perhaps no more than five minutes. From the head of the casket, you will read Scripture, commit the body to the grave, and offer prayer.

Words of the committal are found in directories of worship. While reading these words, I place my hand on the casket.

If the deceased is a military veteran, the flag that draped the coffin will be folded by the honor guard and presented to the spouse or other family member. After the benediction, step forward and shake hands with or hug the members of the family seated in front. When that is completed, the funeral director will announce that the service is concluded.

If there has not been a service at the church or funeral home, the graveside service may include words of remembrance and a brief sermon.

After the Funeral

Immediately following the death of a loved one, the grieving family makes many decisions, meets with comforters, and feels the support of a caring church and community. Calls and meals continue for a time. But this flurry of attention ebbs and ends. After a few weeks, the widow may be left alone with her thoughts, her heart still weighed down by sorrow. The deceased's family is still hurting. Your church may have moved on, but the grieving family has not. Nor should you.

Stay in touch with the family in the coming months. Take note when they experience their first holiday, birthday, or anniversary without their loved one. Anniversaries of deaths are particularly painful. Mark them on your calendar. Older believers may want you to take them to the cemetery on the anniversary of their child's or spouse's death.

There is still work to be done *after* the funeral. You will be staying in touch with family members. Ensure that your elders and other caregivers in your congregation continue to offer their support.

Conclusion

I fear that funerals, as a shared experience of the congregation, are becoming rare. Often the service includes only family and close friends. So it's my practice to encourage the entire church to attend, with the exception of very small children. Of course, this is not always possible; many factors work against our gathering together. Nevertheless, it remains my goal. If the celebration of a birth is a time to rejoice with those who rejoice, then a funeral is the time to grieve with those who grieve. The life of the church is strengthened when we stand together in joys and in sorrows. Work hard to make funerals a gathering of the entire church family.

"No man over-estimates the blessings of peace and concord in all the relations of life. . . . Nor until he sacrifices truth, honor, righteousness or a good conscience does he ever pay too much for them."

—WILLIAM S. PLUMER[14]

15

Your Denominational Duties

OBJECTIVE: To know how to serve your denomination with skill and grace.

IT'S A TRAGEDY that the word *churchman* is disappearing from our vocabulary. A churchman's commitment begins, but does not end, with the local church. He cherishes the church's doctrine, guards its well-being, and promotes its work locally, regionally, and globally. His concern is not only for his own denomination, but also for all true branches of the visible church throughout the world.

During your first year of ministry, begin to build a reputation as a churchman. Most pastors have obligations to ecclesiastical gatherings or assemblies beyond the local church. Serve when asked; serve where needed. Opportunities won't be hard to find.

These meetings of the larger church should be taken seriously. We owe it to God, for we have vowed to the Lord to support the work of his church to the best of our ability. And we owe it to our fellow pastors, for we are colaborers. Thomas Murphy reminds us: "Our fellow-members have a right to our presence and assistance. . . . We wrong them when we stay away. We desert them in their troubles, their toils and their hopes, and we keep from them that portion of aid which we might render."[1]

Here's my advice for your first year of ministry:

Report for Duty

Notify the appropriate person in your ecclesiastical body that you are ready to serve. Cheerfully accept whatever committee assignment is given to you. Don't plead that you are too busy; all ministers are busy and must learn how to balance and discharge the various responsibilities of their office. As work is assigned to you, do it promptly. We devalue our fellow workers when our tardiness holds up business or when the poor quality of our work delays the completion of projects.

Concentrate

Arrive on time for meetings, pay attention to discussion, and don't leave before the end of the business session. Sometimes there are emergencies that require you to leave a meeting early, but these should be few. Good ecclesiastical manners mean staying at your post until work is completed.

Prepare

Study all read-aheads. The agenda and communications should be reviewed before the meeting. If you come unprepared, you won't be able to keep up with the pace of business or weigh the merits of issues to be decided. Never ask for work to slow down because you failed to prepare properly.

---

1. Thomas Murphy, *Pastoral Theology: The Pastor in the Various Duties of His Office* (Whitefish, MT: Kessinger Publishing, 2002), 472.

Get the Fundamentals Right

Your denomination's book of order and parliamentary rules, when understood and used properly, facilitate fair and efficient meetings. Learn how to make a motion. Ministers embarrass themselves when they don't know how to get business before an assembly. This communicates to laymen that they don't take their work seriously, that learning to do things right isn't worth the time, and that good order is unimportant. Laymen should judge you as a person who takes ecclesiastical work as seriously as they do their own business interests.

Don't Be a Jack-in-the-Box

Speak only when you have something that will contribute to the matter before the assembly. Speak too often, and you will become a nuisance. You also risk keeping someone from the floor whose opinion needs to be heard. Murphy warns about ministers who "seem to think that nothing can be rightly transacted unless they have a voice in it."[2] Don't let that be you.

Remember Your Christian Manners

Manners matter. We are brothers in Christ, and should strive to be as kind to one another as possible. Sadly, Murphy observes, "there are some persons who seem to lose their Christian spirit and temper as soon as they engage in public discussions. They enter upon them in a wrangling and angry manner, and at once render the exercise of calm, Christian wisdom impossible. Such a spirit is utterly inconsistent with the character which should be found in Christ's servants. . . .

2. Ibid., 483.

Each one, as he has opportunity should strive to banish angry strifes. . . . It is like *men* to resent opposition, but it is like *Christ* to bear it."[3]

When the Meeting Ends, Guard Your Tongue

Controversy is an inevitable part of Christian life, and especially so when ministers gather. Convictions are strong, and opinions are deeply held. It's always a temptation to speak poorly of those with whom we disagree. Whether we intend to or not, we can slip into habits of conversation that demean our fellow pastors.

I find the advice of Charles Simeon (1759–1836) helpful. To fight against the temptation to speak evil of others, Simeon formulated a strategy. In a July 1817 letter, he counseled:

> The longer I live, the more I feel the importance of adhering to the rules which I have laid down for myself in relation to such matters.
>
> 1st To hear as little as possible what is to the prejudice of others.
>
> 2nd To believe nothing of the kind till I am absolutely forced to it.
>
> 3rd Never to drink into the spirit of one who circulates an ill report.
>
> 4th Always to moderate, as far as I can, the unkindness which is expressed towards others.

3. Ibid., 485–86.

5th Always to believe, that if the other side were heard a very different account would be given of the matter.

I consider love as wealth; and as I would resist a man who should come to rob my house so would I a man who would weaken my regard for any human being.[4]

Our fellow ministers should trust that after meetings, when we go our separate ways, we are careful with each other's reputations.

Encourage Your Fellow Pastors

Write, call, and visit your brothers. Pastoral ministry can be lonely and discouraging, and what a gift you can be to your brothers by being there for them. Ministers especially need your concern after times of failure. Occasionally a governing body must discipline a minister. These are particularly trying times, leaving everyone physically and emotionally drained. If a brother is rebuked for a sin or suspended from his office, he needs your sympathy, compassion, and prayers. Reach out to him.

Keep Your Congregation Involved

Most worship services include an extended prayer for the needs of God's church. Pray for area ministers and their churches. If the churches in your region band together for the planting of new churches, pray for them and pray for conversions.

4. Quoted in Hugh Evan Hopkins, *Charles Simeon of Cambridge* (Grand Rapids: Eerdmans, 1977), 134.

Conclusion

Timothy Dwight wrote of the church:

> For her my tears shall fall,
> For her my prayers ascend;
> To her my cares and toils be giv'n,
> Till toils and cares shall end.[5]

Strive to make that your practice.

---

5. Timothy Dwight, "I Love Thy Kingdom, Lord" (1800), in *Trinity Hymnal,* rev. ed. (Suwanee, GA: Great Commission Publications, 1990), no. 353.

"We should bear in mind, that the honour of God is greatly affected by our conduct; and that our fellow-creatures also may either be 'won by our good conversation,' or be eternally ruined by our misconduct. We should, from these considerations, take especial care never to lay a stumbling-block in the way of others; but so to walk, that we may be able to say unto all around us, 'Whatsoever ye have seen and heard in me, do; and the God of peace shall be with you.'"

—CHARLES SIMEON[15]

"A man who cannot persuade himself to be holy, will have little hope of succeeding with the consciences of others."

—CHARLES BRIDGES[16]

"For a minister to preach the word without constant prayer for its success is a likely means to cherish and strengthen secret atheism in his own heart, and very unlikely to work holiness in the lives of others."

—JOHN OWEN[17]

"Do you not know that in a race all the runners run, but only one receives the prize? So run that you may obtain it. Every athlete exercises self-control in all things. They do it to receive a perishable wreath, but we an imperishable. So I do not run aimlessly; I do not box as one beating the air. But I discipline my body and keep it under control, lest after preaching to others I myself should be disqualified."

—1 CORINTHIANS 9:24–27

"Keep a close watch on yourself and on the teaching. Persist in this, for by so doing you will save both yourself and your hearers."

—1 TIMOTHY 4:16

16

The Character and Habits
of Effective Ministers

OBJECTIVE: To identify and cultivate the character and habits of faithful ministers.

PERSONAL PIETY IS an indispensable requirement of godly and effective ministry. But personal piety alone is not enough. It cannot compensate for lack of discipline. In this chapter, I consider both the holy character *and* the habits you will need to cultivate in your first year of ministry.

Study

Without disciplined habits of study, you will have little new to say. In addition to not nourishing your own soul, your sermons will become repetitive, predictable, and stale. Moreover, your understanding of God's Word and world will prove inadequate to meet the challenges of ministry in a rapidly changing world.

Disciplined study is a must, so plan your study time. Otherwise, it succumbs to the tyranny of the urgent. Shedd recommends five hours of study at the start of the day.[1] When I began my ministry, respected older ministers advised me to study until lunch and then start visiting. It's sound strategy, albeit difficult to implement.

Now consider what to study.

Read the Bible

I assume you're reading the Bible. Although I can point to no commandment written in stone, it does seem prudent for ministers to read the entire Bible at least once a year. I recommend the practice. This is not legalistic. A minister must know the Scriptures, and without a plan to read the Bible regularly and frequently, he won't. It doesn't matter which plan you use; it matters that you have a plan and follow it. For most of my adult life, I have used Robert Murray M'Cheyne's Bible Reading Calendar.

Many men come to seminary without a solid foundation in the Scriptures. They arrive without the benefit of family Bible readings, high school and college Bible courses, and the model of a strong expository pulpit ministry. If this describes you, don't be discouraged. But do recognize that hard work is ahead of you, and don't let your Bible reading slack off during seminary. If you have a wife and children, read aloud to them in addition to your own devotional readings.

An additional word about reading aloud: Many young ministers fumble Scripture readings in worship because they don't practice reading the text. Reading aloud in your study prepares you to read Scripture publicly. Moreover, your understanding of the text will increase, and you will avoid

---

1. William G. T. Shedd, *Homiletics and Pastoral Theology* (New York: Charles Scribner's Sons, 1902), 368.

the temptation to skim and hurry through. Give it a try for a month, and see if it makes a difference.

Other Reading

Choose carefully whatever else you read. Quality is more important than quantity. Don't skim books! You end up with unprocessed information, of little or no use to you or to your congregation.

To read is important; to read with understanding, much more so. Charles Bridges counsels: "No man can read everything; nor would our real store be increased by the capacity to do so. The digestive powers would be overloaded, for want of time to act, and uncontrolled confusion would reign within. It is far more easy to furnish our library, than our understanding." Therefore, Bridges argues, the quality of what we read is more important than the quantity, and for reading to have its greatest value, it must have as its companions "reflection, conversation, and composition."[2]

Make sure that your Christian-reading diet is not pop Christian best sellers. Few of these are theologically reflective, and even fewer will stand the test of time. C. S. Lewis was on to something when he advised, "It is a good rule, after reading a new book, never to allow yourself another new one till you have read an old one in between. If that is too much for you, you should at least read one old one to every three new ones."[3] Some suggestions:

- Study church history. Church history provides a historical perspective on contemporary issues. As you read, you

2. Charles Bridges, *The Christian Ministry: With an Inquiry into the Causes of Its Inefficiency* (Carlisle, PA: Banner of Truth, 1991), 46–47.

3. C. S. Lewis, *God in the Dock: Essays on Theology and Ethics* (Grand Rapids:

will find inspiring examples of faith and courage, as well as beneficial warnings against pride and declension. Your storehouse of weighty sermon illustrations will grow, too.

- Inspirational stories of Christians and churches are often found in secular histories. For example, the American civil-rights movement is filled with stories of Christian courage, as well as tragic Christian obstinacy, cowardice, and compromise.[4]

- Read the biographies and autobiographies of ministers and missionaries. There has not been a time in my ministry when I have not been reading at least one. As you read, you walk with those who faced the same joys and sorrows, victories and conflicts as you—there is much wisdom and inspiration to gain from them.

- Read systematic theology. One of the best gifts you can give your congregation is an understanding of how the great truths of the Christian faith fit together. As you read the confessional standards of the Reformation and the great systematics that followed, your grasp of theology will continue to increase.

- Seek to understand your culture. Read books and subscribe to journals that offer substantial critiques of American life.

- Read poetry and classic literature—for pleasure, for understanding of life, and for learning the power and beauty of the English language. The most important language for you to master is English. It's the language you use to preach and teach God's Word.

Eerdmans, 1970), 201–2.

4. For an overview of the American civil-rights movement in the 1950s and 1960s, see Taylor Branch's magisterial three-volume history: *Parting the Waters: America in the King Years 1954–63* (New York: Simon & Schuster, 1988), *Pillar of Fire: America in the King Years 1963–65* (New York: Simon & Schuster, 1998), and *At Canaan's Edge: America in the King Years 1965–68* (New York: Simon & Schuster, 2006).

- Don't neglect serious novels. A good novelist takes you into the internal lives of his characters. You will find remarkable insights into human nature and the complexities and mysteries of life.
- Enjoy conversations with other ministers over topics of mutual interest.

Pray

Charles Bridges cuts to the heart of Christian ministry when he writes that it "is a work of faith; and, that it may be a work of faith, it must be a work of prayer. Prayer obtains faith, while faith in its reaction quickens to increasing earnestness in prayer."[5]

I take for granted that you are a man of prayer. You shouldn't be in the ministry if you're not. I also take for granted that you pray daily for your family and your church. What I want to encourage here is for you to pray for yourself. Ask God to grant you four virtues that you will need throughout your ministry, especially during your first year:

Pray for patience. Every new minister will find much that he believes needs fixing in his church. So will you. My advice is to be patient and don't rush. Be patient because it takes time to understand your new congregation and the way change takes place in it. Respect the congregation by taking pains to understand them.

For example, I have watched pastors cripple their ministry by changing the order of worship right out of the starting gate. This is poor judgment. First understand how the church came to worship the way it does. Ask questions and listen carefully.

Also be patient because your assessment of the situation

5. Bridges, *The Christian Ministry*, 63.

may change. That has happened to me many times. For example, the pastoral prayer is an important part of worship, and I prefer to offer it. It paves the way for the preaching of the Word, and helps put me in the right frame of mind. When I took a church where the elders insisted on offering that prayer, I chose not to make it an issue. I put myself in the prayer rotation, taking my turn when it came up. Later I planned to ask for change and to assume sole responsibility for the pastoral prayer.

Over time, however, I began to appreciate the church's tradition and eventually supported it. Many male visitors to the church commented that it was impressive to hear men like them offering rich, biblical prayers. Had I acted immediately and pushed for change, I would have deprived the congregation of the nourishing prayers of its elders. Moreover, I would have set the stage for potential conflict.

You will also need patience because people must be led, not pushed and shoved. It takes time to build trust. Begin by respecting the church's leaders. If you have an idea that you believe will advance the work of your church, put it on the agenda for an elders' meeting. Make your case. Let your brothers discuss it. Don't get in a hurry and demand a decision. Give them time to buy into your proposal. If they don't, now is not the time. Be willing, too, to be persuaded by your brothers.

You and your wife will need patience in making new friends. Sometimes a pastor and his wife fit right in with their new church. They like you, and you like them. You feel like you have known them forever.

In another church, you might find people reserved, hesitant to engage you in meaningful conversation, and seemingly indifferent to you, your family, and your ministry. Why?

You could conclude that you have fallen into the hands of the most calloused congregation in Christendom. There are, however, more likely explanations. There may be an age gap.

Especially in small, rural churches, you may serve where there are not many members your age. That was my case early in ministry. There was no one my age in any of the six churches I served as a student pastor. Three positives emerged:

First, I learned to enjoy the companionship of older believers. Intergenerational friendships contributed to my maturity, and forced me to listen to people I would not have chosen to spend as much time with if peer friendships had been immediately available. Some young pastors and their wives have found much-needed second "parents" in their first church, as older couples helped them navigate the early stresses of pastoral ministry, marriage, and raising children.

Second, I formed friendships with pastors of other denominations. My denomination is one small branch of the Christian family. Enjoying the fellowship of brothers in other Christian traditions is something I might have missed but for the need of friendships outside my own congregations.

Finally, lack of peers made me step up my outreach game. In one church, I invited two young men to attend. They did, and became among my closest friends. For a time, I even took up that most frustrating of sports, golf, in order to enjoy their companionship. They became a part of my congregation.

Going to a place where friendships don't come easy is difficult to take, especially if you and your wife have always been popular. Previously, you selected your friends based on mutual interests, values, and goals. Now you find yourself mixing with people who are very different from you, many of whom you would never have shared time with, much less developed close friendships with. For the first time in your life, you must learn the art of building friendships and of learning to value and prize the companionship of people who will bring perspectives to your life that would never have been yours otherwise.

As you strive to become a more patient man, don't forget

that some problems are impervious to solutions. That's the way life is in a fallen world. Bear in mind the words of Cyprian: "Let a man mercifully correct what he can; let him patiently bear what he cannot correct, and groan and sorrow over it with love."[6]

Pray for contentment. French Protestant pastor and poet Antoine de Chandieu (1534–91) warned against the worldly spirit that is never satisfied:

> Never having and always desiring,
> Such are the consequences for him who loves the world.
> The more he abounds in honor and riches,
> The more he is seen aspiring for more.
> He does not enjoy what belongs to him:
> He wants, he values, he adores what other people have.
> When he has everything, it is then that he has nothing.
> Because having everything, he desires everything still.[7]

Learning to be content with your salary may be a challenge in your first church. The pay may be poor. My annual pay was $6,000 before taxes at my first four churches, which were congregations I served simultaneously as a student pastor. Even for a single guy in 1980, that wasn't much. So I worked a man's tobacco field and slopped his hogs in exchange for room and board. It wasn't the way I had planned to start my ministry. Quickly I became friends with the farmer's wonderful family and, in a community of farmers, earned a modest degree of respect. It wasn't the path I would have chosen, but the Lord provided just what I needed.

---

6. Quoted in Scott M. Manetsch, *Calvin's Company of Pastors: Pastoral Care and the Emerging Reformed Church, 1536–1609* (New York: Oxford University Press, 2013), 189.

7. Quoted in ibid., 98.

Churches are assemblies of God's dear people, not stepping-stones. Don't look on them as nuisances on your way to a better position. If you do, your ministry is likely to end sooner rather than later—and in disappointment.

Pray for the power to forgive. A good pastor is in close contact with his flock, and this provides many opportunities for careless words, severe judgments, conflict, and hurt. Many times when there is a change in pastoral leadership, the new pastor arrives to find that some folks won't give him a chance. In one of my churches, a woman told me matter-of-factly that she and her husband considered me a step down from the intellectual caliber of the previous pastor, and that they would be transferring to another church. It's easy to get angry. Add to the mix your sins and shortcomings, and things can swiftly go awry.

Here's my advice: learn to own up to your sins promptly and repent quickly. And when wronged, forgive from the heart— and forgive before you're asked. Ask the Lord for the power to put aside all wrath and malice and bitterness. You must crucify sinful anger. A pastor can be angry with people, and he can effectively minister the gospel of God's grace. But it's one or the other. No man can minister God's grace effectively while angry with his flock. Seek counsel. Wrestle in prayer. Do whatever it takes to get rid of the anger and get on with ministry.

Pray for gentleness. Paul describes his care for the new believers in the church at Thessalonica: "But we were gentle among you, like a nursing mother taking care of her own children" (1 Thess. 2:7). The nursing mother's concern is not for herself, but for her child, who is wholly dependent upon her for care and feeding. The child does not serve his mother; she serves him. Paul functioned as a nursing mother among the Thessalonians, seeking their interests, not his own, and pursuing their growth in Christ, not his own glory or financial profit. He devoted himself exclusively to caring for the church—newborn babes in Christ—and to their nourishment in God's Word.

The key word is *gentle*. God's servant must not be harsh, overbearing, or intimidating. Instead, he approaches his flock with "the meekness and gentleness of Christ" (2 Cor. 10:1). Gentleness is a fruit of God's Holy Spirit that is present in every true believer and especially evident in those who lead (Gal. 5:23). If I could do my ministry all over again, this is what I would wish for the most: more Christlike gentleness at home, among the congregation, and in the courts of the church.

Seize Small Bits of Time

Twenty, ten, or even five minutes are valuable and can be put to profitable use. Don't look at your watch, see that you have only a few minutes until your next appointment, and fritter the time away by daydreaming or mindlessly surfing the Internet. Small bits of time add up, especially over a lifetime.

With customary bluntness, Shedd writes: "Small spaces of time become ample and great by being regularly and faithfully employed. It is because time is wasted so regularly and uniformly, and not because it is wasted in such large amounts, that so much of human life runs to waste."[8]

Wherever I go, I carry a book or note cards. The minutes of downtime add up, and it's astounding how much can be read or written.

When There's a Pastoral Emergency, Be There

Run to those in need. The shepherd's eyes are open to the needs of his sheep, especially to the injured, weak, and frightened.

---

8. Shedd, *Homiletics and Pastoral Theology*, 394.

Genevan minister Theodore Beza (1519–1605) describes beautifully the responsibilities of the Christian pastor:

> It is not only necessary that [a pastor] have a general knowledge of his flock, but he must also know and call each of his sheep by name, both in public and in their homes, both night and day. Pastors must run after lost sheep, bandaging up the one with a broken leg, strengthening the one that is sick. . . . In sum, the pastor must consider his sheep more dear to him than his own life, following the example of the Good Shepherd.[9]

Take Care of Your Body

Pay attention to rest. Ministry is demanding. You need sleep, breaks *from* your study, breaks *for* study, and vacations. I check with my pastoral staff (and that includes spouses) to ensure that they are taking the full allotment of time that the church gives them to be away from the church for rest, refreshment, and study. Attention to this is requisite for long-term success. Solo pastors have no supervisors, so make sure you take care of yourself and your family by getting sufficient rest from your ministerial labors.

Exercise. I don't mean extreme sports. Only running, walking, swimming, or whatever you do to keep your body fit. Do more, if you are so inclined. But at the very least, take care of the body that God has given you.

Put Your Family on the Calendar

Reserve nights and other times to be with your wife and children. Put your children's important events on your

---

9. Quoted in Manetsch, *Calvin's Company of Pastors*, 281.

schedule. Emergencies and crises will come, and you'll have to be ready to be there for your congregation. That's understandable; that comes with your call to ministry.

What is inexcusable is to permit routine ministerial duties—committee meetings, pastoral visitation, administrative work, and sermon preparation—to take you away from time with your family. Schedule time to be with family, and when you are, give them your full attention. Put away the computer and smartphone. Focus on the folks at hand—the most important sheep in the flock—your family.

Conclusion

Your first church is the place to establish habits that will increase your effectiveness in lifelong service to Christ's church. Reflect on the disciplines you will need for the long haul, and make acquiring them a nonnegotiable priority.

"It is a troubled, tangled world in which we are living now; and God knows there is enough darkness in it without our doing anything, by dullness or depression or sullen cynicism, to make that darkness deeper. The real servant of humanity today is the man whose life breathes praise."

—JAMES S. STEWART[18]

17

Small Things That Yield Big Results

OBJECTIVE: To identify small things that, when practiced over time, can yield big results in your ministry.

SMALL THINGS WILL yield big results during your first year of ministry. Don't discount them. Keep your eyes open for acts of caring that will build trust and goodwill between you and your flock.

In no particular order, here are some small things that have proved valuable to my ministry. Perhaps you will find them useful, too.

Welcome People at the Door and Say Good-bye to Them as They Leave

Arriving at church early, greeting the flock by name, and asking about their week lets people know that you're glad to see them. If you find that this leaves you distracted and unready to begin worship, then don't do it. However, my experience has been that welcoming people increases mutual affection. It is always gratifying when other members catch on, arrive early, and greet with me—especially when they welcome visitors warmly. Lead the way in making your congregation a welcoming church!

I prefer to greet people outside the church building. What if it's cold and snowing? Dress warmly. What if it's raining? Take a large umbrella and help people out of their cars and get them inside. You're there to serve.

Ten minutes before the service begins, I take my seat behind the pulpit and collect my thoughts. Five minutes before the service, I ask the congregation to quiet themselves before the Lord. I find this is a good balance between welcoming and preparation for worship.

As people leave the place of worship, say good-bye. Let them know that you're glad they were there. If you can't communicate this with integrity, repent and change your attitude. These are dear folks whom God has entrusted to your care. Love them!

I keep a notebook in my pocket. During these brief exchanges before and after church, people share important news in passing—a sickness, a trial, or a reason to give thanks. Write down the information and follow up with a phone call—don't trust your memory.

Send Birthday Notes

Cards are fine, but handwritten notes are even better. In birthday notes, I wish my members a happy birthday and give thanks for virtues I see in their lives. You encourage others when you recognize God's work in their lives. Some parents save my cards and reread them to their children each year. Letters—unlike phone calls and more than emails—can be saved and treasured.

I believe that I have every letter ever written to me. Whenever I move and reduce the number of my files, I look through these letters again. The care that people have taken to encourage me has meant so much. I want others to be as encouraged as I have been.

Send Congratulatory Notes

Find where awards are posted, in newspapers or Facebook or wherever, and call or write to acknowledge them. We must rejoice with those who rejoice.

Remember the Children

Know the children of your congregation by name. It's inexcusable not to—they are precious lambs in your flock. The Lord knows their names, and you should, too. If you don't take the time to know them and greet them by name, it suggests two things, both blameworthy: you don't care about them and aren't praying for them.

Celebrate the achievements of your church's children. Attend games, concerts, and award ceremonies. You will encourage the children, and (especially at sporting events) you will have ample time to talk with parents.

Think in Terms of Community

Your congregation is situated within a community. Become part of its life by joining civic clubs, volunteer associations, boards, book clubs, and other venues that bring people together.

Some of the people you meet may become part of your church. But more importantly, your presence reveals your concern for the well-being of all of God's image-bearers and for the community in which God has placed you. You will also meet professional people who can offer you needed advice and to whom you can refer congregants.

Visit Area Churches

On my vacation Sundays (when I am in town), I visit other local churches, including those that are not part of my denomination. Learn what's going on in the broader Christian community. Introduce yourself to other pastors. Friendships with them will provide mutual encouragement, as well as helping you to understand your community. Take the initiative. Call and schedule lunch or coffee meetings.

Talk to Strangers

When you're in a checkout line or milling around waiting for a meeting to start, put away the smartphone and talk to people. I have gained church members and staff just by paying attention to those around me.

Once, while in a grocery line, I heard a woman ask the cashier if the store had any boxes. No, he said, the trash had been collected earlier in the day. Butting in, I said that I had recently moved and that my boxes were hers for the taking. She waited for me to check out and followed me home. We talked. It turned out that she was an organist. She visited my church, and soon I had a new organist.

What a joy it was on another occasion to meet a young couple at a civic group's meet-and-greet. They visited our church, and several months later I baptized them upon their public professions of faith in Christ.

Back in the old days, when UPS deliveries required a signature, the young driver asked me why so many boxes were delivered to my apartment. "I'm a pastor and pastors love books. Do you have a church home?" "No," he replied. "Then please pay us a visit," I urged. He did, and several months later both he and his wife professed faith and were baptized.

Have Fun

In 2005, I returned south to Huntsville, Alabama, near the part of Tennessee I call home. Many of the places where I hiked, camped, canoed, and caved were close by, so I founded a church hiking club to take folks on day trips to enjoy the natural beauty of north Alabama and southern Middle Tennessee. I enjoyed many hours of relaxing conversation with people I love.

Whatever you enjoy doing, find a way to involve your congregation if it will deepen relationships and strengthen friendships.

Conclusion

Little things that we do without thinking—like talking to someone in a checkout line or sending a birthday note—can yield abundant fruit in your ministry. Become intentional about making them a way of life.

"I have fought the good fight, I have finished the race, I have kept the faith. Henceforth there is laid up for me the crown of righteousness, which the Lord, the righteous judge, will award to me on that Day, and not only to me but also to all who have loved his appearing."

—2 TIMOTHY 4:7–8

18

A Long and Fruitful Ministry

OBJECTIVE: To plan and carry out your ministry with the end in view.

I WANT EACH of you to have a long and fruitful ministry. For that to happen, many things must take place. I'll concentrate on two.

First, for a long and fruitful ministry, you must intercede for your congregation in your secret prayers.

Secret prayer is the time you spend alone with the Lord—pouring out your heart for the congregation he has called you to serve and seeking those graces you must have if you're to serve them well.

Without secret prayer, there can be no real Christian ministry. That's why Bishop Moule sought to impress upon his ministerial students that "the heart of the minister's life is the man's Secret Communion with God."[1]

Nothing will build stronger bonds of affection with your congregation than praying earnestly for them.

In prayer, we come before the throne of grace, pleading

---

1. H. C. G. Moule, *To My Younger Brethren: Chapters on Pastoral Life and Work* (London: Hodder and Stoughton, 1892), 23.

with God to grant grace to the sick, comfort to the mourner, strength to the weak, certainty to the doubting, clarity to the confused, and hope to the despairing.

In prayer, we also seek God's sanctifying grace for our people. They must be holy as he is holy, for without holiness, no man shall see the Lord (1 Peter 1:16; Heb. 12:14). "Blessed are the pure in heart, for they shall see God" (Matt. 5:8). Your people face many urgent temporal concerns, and you must intercede for them, but of critical importance is each member's personal holiness, his Christlikeness. The name of the Lord must be honored in the godly behavior and godly doctrine of his flock—and this must be your principal concern.

In your prayers for your congregation, you pray also for the graces that you need to be faithful in your ministerial calling. Soundness of doctrine, holiness of life, a zeal to reach the lost, a willingness to bear the burdens of your congregation, perseverance in affliction—whatever you need, make it a matter of prayer. "Keep a close watch on yourself and on the teaching. Persist in this, for by so doing you will save both yourself and your hearers" (1 Tim. 4:16).

The frequency and intensity of our prayers for ourselves and for our congregations are known only to us and to God. Yet I doubt there is any greater measure of ministerial godliness. If we attempt to carry on a ministry without earnestly praying for our congregations, then we will find ourselves on perilous ground.

Why is that? Why is a ministry without private prayer spiritually deadly? Because when we fail to pray, we reveal ourselves to be hypocrites. We minister in Christ's name without personal communion with him.

Alexander Whyte raises this very point in *Bunyan Characters*. In his lecture on "Formalist and Hypocrisy," he writes of the hypocritical minister sweating at his sermons and in his visiting, till you would almost think that he is the minister of whom Paul prophesied, who should spend and be spent for the salvation of men's souls. But all the time, such is the hypocrisy that haunts the ministerial calling, he is really and at bottom animated with ambition for the praise of men only, and for the increase of his congregation.[2]

What exposes Hypocrite's heart is the absence of secret prayer. That mustn't be you!

Secret prayer for our flocks that is frequent and intense indicates a heart for God and a heart for the people of God. Without it, there is never long and fruitful ministry.

And that's what I want for you—a long and fruitful ministry. For that to happen, you must intercede for your congregation in your secret prayers.

And, next, you must speak affectionately both *to* your congregation and *about* your congregation.

Remember Paul's experience in Thessalonica. After a ministry that lasted only a month, he was forced from the city, leaving behind a church full of new converts. The pain of separation was real, and the anguish of the troubled Thessalonians could not be ignored. So with moving words, Paul reassured them by letter of his abiding love and affection, asking, "For what is our hope or joy or crown of boasting before our Lord Jesus at his coming?" (1 Thess. 2:19a).

What a question! I can imagine the letter being read to the Thessalonians for the first time. The reader of the letter asks Paul's question: "What is our hope or joy or crown of boasting before our Lord Jesus at his coming?" He pauses and

---

2. Alexander Whyte, *Bunyan Characters*, vol. 1 (Eugene, OR: Wipf and Stock Publishers, 2000), 138.

gives the congregation time to mull it over. Then comes Paul's answer: "Is it not you? For you are our glory and joy" (1 Thess. 2:19b–20).

Paul's crown of boasting is saved Thessalonian believers whom he will present to the Lord at his coming. They are his glory and joy. Paul spoke affectionately of believers he loved. So should you.

One of the finest elders I've ever known taught me a valuable lesson. He never did something that is so common among Christian parents: complain about our kids, even exaggerating their faults, in order to get sympathy or even a laugh. Without ever bragging, he talked about his children only with respect, pride, and gratitude. And his children adored him. Affectionate words showed just how much he cared for them.

Listen to your speech. How do you talk to your congregation when you're in the pulpit? How do your members feel while sharing conversation with you? Do they sense your deep affection for them?

And how do you talk about your congregation when they are absent? When you're with fellow ministers or with your wife or alone with your own thoughts, what do you say? Wherever you are, speak of them with tenderness and warmth.

If you begin to speak otherwise, catch yourself, repent, and from the heart talk about them with deepest affection.

Then in your heart and speech they will be your glory and joy. And you will be well down the road to a long and fruitful ministry.

APPENDIX 1

Advice for Student Preachers

I AM THE director of field education at Reformed Theological Seminary in Jackson, Mississippi. Each week students from the seminary head to church to lead worship and preach. These are my guidelines:

A. Dress Appropriately
   1. Wear a coat and tie.
   2. Take two handkerchiefs with you—one for you and one for someone else if the need arises.

B. Family
   1. Your children must be under control during the service.
   2. If your family attends, strive to enjoy the time of worship.

C. Procedure
   1. Reach out to the church ahead of time. Through your contact person, find out something about the church. They will appreciate your effort.
   2. Arrive at church at least forty-five minutes ahead of time. Research directions a few days in advance and plan your trip.

3. Take and use breath mints. We don't notice our own stale-coffee breath, but others do.
4. Make sure to stand at the door and greet people. You will want to welcome them to worship and shake their hands.
5. If you are offered hospitality, accept it.
6. Be aware of the community's cultural values. Don't needlessly offend.
7. Send handwritten thank-you notes to show appreciation for the opportunity to preach and for any hospitality received.
8. Always remember that you are representing the Lord, your church, your family, and your seminary.
9. Greet the children and learn their names.
10. Write down the names of those you meet. Memorize them before you return.

D. During the Service
1. Do not worry about low attendance.
2. Do not use coarse language or profanity in or out of the pulpit. You are a man of God.
3. Do not read your sermon.

E. After the Service and Follow-Up
1. At the end of the service, go to the door and thank everyone for coming.
2. Express gratitude to those to whom you minister.
3. Accept feedback with sincere thanks.
4. It is never your role as a circuit preacher to adjudicate church disputes.

APPENDIX 2

Tips for Seeking a Pastoral Position

1. Don't procrastinate. Become a candidate for ministry in your denomination as early as possible. Follow your candidates committee's instructions to a tee.

Don't put off candidacy and its requirements until the end of your seminary career. If you do, you will complete your seminary requirements, but be unready to accept a call because you've failed to submit to your denomination's ordination requirements. That may mean you are many months away from accepting a call. Show respect for your denomination and love for your family by staying on track.

PCA students need to keep the following in mind:

- You must be a member for at least six months of a church in the presbytery where you want to come under care.
- You must also be endorsed by the session of that church before it is possible to become a candidate and intern.
- Before ordination, you must complete a presbytery internship, which must last at least twelve months.
- The process to be ready to be ordained requires a minimum of eighteen months to complete and, for most candidates, is closer to thirty months.

2. Prepare your résumé carefully. Proofread it, and get someone else to proofread it also. Expect your prospective employer to verify each detail. Be accurate. The care with which you prepare your résumé is one indicator of the care you will take with the work that your future church entrusts to you.

3. Circulate your résumé widely. Ask minister friends whether they know of openings. Not every position is listed on your denomination's website, and some positions may be coming open and are not yet announced.

4. Compose a cover letter (or email). Attach to each résumé a cover letter addressed to the person or committee responsible for receiving your résumé. Tailor each cover letter to the position. Proofread it, and get someone else to proofread it also. Ask a friend in business to critique your cover letter before you send it. Your cover letter creates your first impression.

5. Include references. Include the names of references in your résumé. Don't make the pulpit committee ask for them. Make sure you have obtained permission to use your references' names, and that their contact information is correct.

6. Keep your résumé current. Double-check all contact information for you and your references.

7. Be thoughtful. Acknowledge all inquiries with a handwritten thank-you note.

8. Be prepared. At interviews, either preliminary or when formally candidating:

- Wear a suit.
- Take two handkerchiefs, one for yourself and one for someone else, if needed. A gentleman is always thinking of others.
- Answer questions as briefly as possible. Don't ramble.
- Answer all questions directly and honestly.
- Ask the pulpit search committee questions and listen intently to their answers. A good pastor is a good listener.

- Sit up straight. Look at people when they speak to you. Manners matter.
- Stand up when ladies enter the room. You are a gentleman.
- Write thank-you notes to the entire pulpit committee. It's an honor to be granted an interview.
- Write thank-you notes to anyone who helps you during your visit. For example, if you're meeting with a committee at someone's office and his assistant gets you a drink while you wait, send the assistant a thank-you note. Acknowledge the kind service to you.
- In emails, use formal elements of style, like "Dear Mr. Adams" and "Yours in Christ, Charlie." Use good grammar. Punctuate properly. Use capital letters at the beginning of a sentence and wherever appropriate. Avoid slang. Check your spelling.

9. Disclose. If you have been under church discipline or have ever had any problems with the law, you need to tell the pulpit search committee. If you fail to disclose this and the committee obtains the information during their reference and background check, they will question your honesty and wonder what else you are withholding. Your candidacy will almost certainly come to an end.

10. Engage people. When you are candidating at a church, speak to everyone—and especially to the children. Learn names.

11. Be grateful. It is an honor to be asked to candidate. Be thankful—to God and the congregation.

12. Treat your wife as your partner. Discuss together, pray together, decide together. You are a team.

Readings in Preaching
and Pastoral Theology

Adams, Jay E. *Preaching with Purpose*. Phillipsburg, NJ: P&R Publishing, 1982; Grand Rapids: Zondervan, 1986.

———. *Shepherding God's Flock*. 3 vols. Grand Rapids: Zondervan, 1974–75.

Alexander, J. W. *Thoughts on Preaching*. Carlisle, PA: Banner of Truth, 1988.

Anyabwile, Thabiti M. *The Faithful Preacher: Recapturing the Vision of Three Pioneering African-American Pastors*. Wheaton, IL: Crossway, 2007.

Ash, Christopher. *The Priority of Preaching*. Ross-shire, UK: Christian Focus, 2010.

Azurdia, Arturo G., III. *Spirit Empowered Preaching: Involving the Holy Spirit in Your Ministry*. Ross-shire, UK: Christian Focus, 1998.

Bannerman, James. *The Church of Christ: A Treatise on the Nature, Powers, Ordinances, Discipline, and Government of the Christian Church*. Edmonton: Still Waters Revival Books, 1991.

Baxter, Richard. *A Christian Directory*. Vol. 1, *The Practical Works of Richard Baxter*. Ligonier, PA: Soli Deo Gloria, 1990.

———. *The Reformed Pastor*. Carlisle, PA: Banner of Truth, 1989.

Bennett, Arthur. *The Valley of Vision*. Carlisle, PA: Banner of Truth, 2003.

Bewes, Richard. *Speaking in Public Effectively*. Ross-shire, UK: Christian Focus, 1998.

Blaikie, William G. *For the Work of the Ministry: A Manual of Homiletical and Pastoral Theology*. Birmingham, AL: Solid Ground Christian Books, 2005.

Bridges, Charles. *The Christian Ministry: With an Inquiry into the Causes of Its Inefficiency*. Carlisle, PA: Banner of Truth, 1991.

Bridges, Jerry. *Respectable Sins: Confronting the Sins We Tolerate*. Colorado Springs: NavPress, 2007.

Broadus, John A. *Lectures on the History of Preaching*. Vestavia Hills, AL: Solid Ground Christian Books, 2004.

————. *On the Preparation and Delivery of Sermons*. Vestavia Hills, AL: Solid Ground Christian Books, 2005.

Brown, Charles. *The Ministry*. Carlisle, PA: Banner of Truth, 2006.

Bucer, Martin. *Concerning the True Care of Souls*. Carlisle, PA: Banner of Truth, 2009.

Bunyan, John. *The Pilgrim's Progress*. Carlisle, PA: Banner of Truth, 2005.

Calhoun, David. *Prayers on the Psalms: From the Scottish Psalter of 1595*. Carlisle, PA: Banner of Truth, 2010.

Campbell, Iain D. *Pray, Plan, Prepare, Preach: Establishing and Maintaining Priorities in the Preaching Ministry*. Leominster, UK: Day One Publications, 2012.

Carson, D. A. *A Call to Spiritual Reformation: Priorities from Paul and His Prayers*. Grand Rapids: Baker, 1992.

————. *The Cross and Christian Ministry: Leadership Lessons from 1 Corinthians*. Grand Rapids: Baker, 1993.

Chapell, Bryan. *Christ-Centered Preaching: Redeeming the Expository Sermon*. Grand Rapids: Baker, 2005.

————. *Christ-Centered Worship: Letting the Gospel Shape Our Practice*. Grand Rapids: Baker, 2009.

————. *Using Illustrations to Preach with Power*. Wheaton, IL: Crossway, 2001.

Charles, H. B., Jr. *On Preaching: Personal and Pastoral Insights for the Preparation and Practice of Preaching*. Chicago: Moody Publishers, 2014.

Chrysostom, St. John. *Six Books on the Priesthood*. Crestwood, NY: St. Vladimir's Seminary Press, 1984.

Clebsch, William A., and Charles Jaekle. *Pastoral Care in Historical Perspective*. New York: Jason Aronson, 1983.

Clowney, Edmund P. *Called to the Ministry*. Phillipsburg, NJ: P&R Publishing, 1976.

————. *Preaching and Biblical Theology*. Phillipsburg, NJ: P&R Publishing, 2002.

————. *Preaching Christ in All of Scripture*. Wheaton, IL: Crossway, 2003.

————. *The Unfolding Mystery: Discovering Christ in the Old Testament*. Colorado Springs: NavPress, 1988.

Croft, Brian. *Visit the Sick: Ministering God's Grace in Times of Illness*. Grand Rapids: Zondervan, 2014.

Dabney, Robert Lewis. *Sacred Rhetoric: or, A Course of Lectures on Preaching*. Whitefish, MT: Kessinger Publishing, 2010.

Dallimore, Arnold. *Spurgeon: A New Biography*. Edinburgh: Banner of Truth, 1985.

Dargan, Edwin Charles. *The History of Preaching*. Grand Rapids: Baker, 1954.

Davis, Bill. *Departing in Peace: Biblical Decision-Making at the End of Life*. Phillipsburg, NJ: P&R Publishing, 2017.

Davis, Dale Ralph. *The Word Became Fresh: How to Preach from Old Testament Narrative Texts*. Ross-shire, UK: Christian Focus, 2006.

Dever, Mark, and Greg Gilbert. *Preach: Theology Meets Practice*. Nashville: B&H, 2012.

Dickson, David. *The Elder and His Work*. Phillipsburg, NJ: P&R Publishing, 2004.

Drucker, Peter F. *The Effective Executive: The Definitive Guide to Getting the Right Things Done*. New York: HarperCollins, 2002.

Eby, David. *Power Preaching for Church Growth: The Role of Preaching in Growing Churches*. Ross-shire, UK: Christian Focus, 1996.

Episcopal Church. *The Book of Common Prayer*. New York: Oxford University Press, 1993.

Fairbairn, Patrick. *Pastoral Theology: A Treatise on the Office and Duties of the Christian Pastor*. Audubon, NJ: Old Paths Publications, 1992.

Garretson, James M. *Princeton and Preaching: Archibald Alexander and the Christian Ministry*. Carlisle, PA: Banner of Truth, 2005.

———. *Princeton and the Work of the Christian Ministry*. 2 vols. Carlisle, PA: Banner of Truth, 2012.

Goldsworthy, Graeme. *Preaching the Whole Bible as Christian Scripture*. Grand Rapids: Eerdmans, 2000.

Gordon, T. David. *Why Johnny Can't Preach: The Media Have Shaped the Messengers*. Phillipsburg, NJ: P&R Publishing, 2009.

———. *Why Johnny Can't Sing Hymns: How Pop Culture Rewrote the Hymnal*. Phillipsburg, NJ: P&R Publishing, 2010.

Gregory the Great. *The Book of Pastoral Rule*. Crestwood, NY: St. Vladimir's Seminary Press, 2007.

Houghton, Elsie. *Classic Christian Hymn-Writers*. Fort Washington, PA: Christian Literature Crusade, 1982.

Hughes, R. Kent, and Barbara Hughes. *Liberating Ministry from the Success Syndrome*. Wheaton, IL: Crossway, 2008.

James, John Angell. *An Earnest Ministry: The Want of the Times*. Carlisle, PA: Banner of Truth, 1993.

Johnson, Dennis E. *Him We Proclaim: Preaching Christ from All the Scriptures*. Phillipsburg, NJ: P&R Publishing, 2007.

Johnson, Terry L., ed. *Leading in Worship*. Rev. ed. White Hall, WV: Tolle Lege Press, 2013.

————. *Reformed Worship: Worship That Is according to Scripture*. Greenville, SC: Reformed Academic Press, 2000.

————. *Worshiping with Calvin: Recovering the Historic Ministry and Worship of Reformed Protestantism*. Darlington, UK: EP Books, 2014.

Jones, Paul S. *Singing and Making Music: Issues in Church Music Today*. Phillipsburg, NJ: P&R Publishing, 2006.

Keller, Timothy. *Preaching: Communicating Faith in an Age of Skepticism*. New York: Viking, 2015.

Kelly, Douglas. *Preachers with Power: Four Stalwarts of the South*. Carlisle, PA: Banner of Truth, 1992.

Kistler, Don, ed. *Feed My Sheep: A Passionate Plea for Preaching*. Orlando, FL: Soli Deo Gloria Publications, 2002.

Lloyd-Jones, D. Martyn. *Preaching and Preachers*. Grand Rapids: Zondervan, 2011.

Macartney, Clarence Edward. *Preaching without Notes*. Nashville: Abingdon, 1946.

Manetsch, Scott M. *Calvin's Company of Pastors: Pastoral Care and the Emerging Reformed Church, 1536–1609*. New York: Oxford University Press, 2013.

Martin, Albert N. *You Lift Me Up: Overcoming Ministry Challenges*. Ross-shire, UK: Christian Focus, 2013.

Massey, James Earl. *The Burdensome Joy of Preaching*. Nashville: Abingdon, 1998.

McNeill, John T. *A History of the Cure of Souls*. New York: Harper & Row, 1951.

Meilaender, Gilbert. *Bioethics: A Primer for Christians*. Grand Rapids: Eerdmans, 2005.

Millar, Gary, and Phil Campbell. *Saving Eutychus: How to Preach God's Word and Keep People Awake*. Kingsford, Australia: Matthias Media, 2013.

Miller, Samuel. *Thoughts on Public Prayer*. Harrisonburg, PA: Sprinkle Publications, 1985.

Motyer, Alec. *Preaching? Simple Teaching on Simply Preaching*. Ross-shire, UK: Christian Focus, 2013.

Murphy, Thomas. *Pastoral Theology: The Pastor in the Various Duties of His Office*. Whitefish, MT: Kessinger Publishing, 2002.

Murray, David P. *Reset: Living a Grace-Paced Life in a Burnout Culture*. Wheaton, IL: Crossway, 2017.

Murray, Shona, and David Murray. *Refresh: Embracing a Grace-Paced Life in a World of Endless Demands*. Wheaton, IL: Crossway, 2017.

Old, Hughes Oliphant. *Leading in Prayer: A Workbook for Ministers*. Grand Rapids: Eerdmans, 1995.

———. *The Reading and Preaching of the Scriptures in the Worship of the Christian Church*. Vol. 4, *The Age of Reformation*. Grand Rapids: Eerdmans, 2002.

———. *Worship: Reformed according to Scripture*. Louisville: Westminster John Knox, 2002.

Olyott, Stuart. *Ministering like the Master: Three Messages for Today's Preachers*. Carlisle, PA: Banner of Truth, 2003.

Orthodox Presbyterian Church. *The Book of Church Order of the Orthodox Presbyterian Church*. Willow Grove, PA: Committee on Christian Education of the Orthodox Presbyterian Church, 2000.

Packer, J. I. *Evangelism and the Sovereignty of God*. Downers Grove, IL: InterVarsity Press, 1961.

Peck, T. E. *Notes on Ecclesiology*. Richmond, VA: Presbyterian Committee of Publication, 1892.

Perkins, William. *The Art of Prophesying*. Carlisle, PA: Banner of Truth, 1996.

Piper, John. *Brothers, We Are Not Professionals: A Plea to Pastors for Radical Ministry*. Nashville: B&H, 2002.

———. *The Supremacy of God in Preaching*. Grand Rapids: Baker, 1990.

Postman, Neil. *Amusing Ourselves to Death: Public Discourse in the Age of Show Business*. New York: Penguin, 1985.

Pratt, Josiah, and John Henry Pratt, eds. *The Thought of the Evangelical Leaders: Notes of the Discussions of the Eclectic Society, London during the Years 1798–1814*. Edinburgh: Banner of Truth, 1978.

Presbyterian Church in America, General Assembly. *The Book of Church Order of the Presbyterian Church in America*. 6th ed. Lawrenceville, GA: Christian Education and Publications, 2013.

———. *The Westminster Confession of Faith and Catechisms: As Adopted by the Presbyterian Church in America*. Lawrenceville, GA: Christian Education and Publications, 2007.

Prime, Derek, and Alistair Begg. *On Being a Pastor: Understanding Our Calling and Work*. Chicago: Moody Publishers, 2004.

Robinson, Haddon W. *Biblical Preaching: The Development and Delivery of Expository Messages*. Grand Rapids: Baker, 2001.

Shaw, James E. *Classic Hymns of Christendom: Fifty-two Stories and Studies of Scripture Which Inspired the Hymns*. Rapid City, SD: Crosslink Publishing, 2013.

Shedd, William G. T. *Homiletics and Pastoral Theology*. New York: Charles Scribner's Sons, 1902.

Short, David, and David Searle. *Pastoral Visitation: A Pocket Manual*. Ross-shire, UK: Christian Focus; Edinburgh: Rutherford House, 2004.

Smith, Morton H. *Commentary on the PCA Book of Church Order*. Taylors, SC: Presbyterian Press, 2007.

Spring, Gardiner. *The Distinguishing Traits of Christian Character*. Phillipsburg, NJ: P&R Publishing, 1967.

———. *The Power of the Pulpit: Thoughts to Christian Ministers and Those Who Hear Them*. Carlisle, PA: Banner of Truth, 1986.

Spurgeon, Charles Haddon. *An All-Round Ministry*. Pasadena, TX: Pilgrim Publications, 1983.

———. *Lectures to My Students*. Carlisle, PA: Banner of Truth, 2008.

———. *The Pastor in Prayer: A Collection of the Sunday Morning Prayers of C. H. Spurgeon*. Carlisle, PA: Banner of Truth, 2004.

Still, William. *Dying to Live*. Ross-shire, UK: Christian Focus, 1991.

———. *The Work of the Pastor*. Rev. ed. Ross-shire, UK: Christian Focus, 2010.

Stott, John R. W. *Between Two Worlds: The Challenge of Preaching Today*. Grand Rapids: Eerdmans, 1982.

———. *The Preacher's Portrait: Some New Testament Word Studies*. Grand Rapids: Eerdmans, 1961.

Von Allmen, Jean-Jacques. *Preaching and Congregation: Ecumenical Studies in Worship*. Richmond: John Knox, 1962.

Warfield, Benjamin B. *The Religious Life of Theological Students*. Phillipsburg, NJ: P&R Publishing, 1983.

Waters, Guy P. *How Jesus Runs the Church*. Phillipsburg, NJ: P&R Publishing, 2011.

Watson, Thomas. *The Godly Man's Picture*. Edinburgh: Banner of Truth, 1992.

Wells, David F. *The Courage to Be Protestant: Truth-Lovers, Marketers, and Emergents in the Postmodern World*. Grand Rapids: Eerdmans, 2008.

White, Peter. *The Effective Pastor: Get the Tools to Upgrade Your Ministry*. Ross-shire, UK: Christian Focus, 2000.

Wiersbe, Warren, and David Wiersbe. *Ministering to the Mourning: A Practical Guide for Pastors, Church Leaders, and Other Caregivers*. Chicago: Moody Publishers, 2006.

Witmer, Timothy. *The Shepherd Leader: Achieving Effective Shepherding in Your Church*. Phillipsburg, NJ: P&R Publishing, 2010.

Witsius, Herman. *On the Character of a True Theologian*. Greenville, SC: Reformed Academic Press, 1994.

Notes

1. Quoted in Thabiti M. Anyabwile, *The Faithful Preacher: Recapturing the Vision of Three Pioneering African-American Pastors* (Wheaton, IL: Crossway, 2007), 82.

2. William Childs Robinson, *The Certainties of the Gospel* (Grand Rapids: Zondervan, 1935), 130.

3. James S. Stewart, *Heralds of God: A Practical Book on Preaching* (Vancouver: Regent, 2001), 189.

4. John Owen, *The Works of John Owen*, ed. William H. Goold, vol. 16 (Edinburgh: T&T Clark, n.d.), 76.

5. William G. Blaikie, *For the Work of the Ministry: A Manual of Homiletical and Pastoral Theology* (Birmingham, AL: Solid Ground Christian Books, 2005), 5.

6. Quoted in R. Albert Mohler Jr., "Expository Preaching: Center of Christian Worship," in *Give Praise to God: A Vision for Reforming Worship*, ed. Philip Graham Ryken, Derek W. H. Thomas, and J. Ligon Duncan III (Phillipsburg, NJ: P&R Publishing, 2003), 112.

7. Hughes Oliphant Old, *Worship: Reformed according to Scripture* (Louisville: Westminster John Knox, 2002), 2.

8. J. Ligon Duncan III, "Does God Care How We Worship?," in *Give Praise to God: A Vision for Reforming Worship*, ed. Philip Graham Ryken, Derek W. H. Thomas, and J. Ligon Duncan III (Phillipsburg, NJ: P&R Publishing, 2003), 35.

9. Westminster Shorter Catechism 92, 93.

10. Ken Sande, *The Peacemaker: A Biblical Guide to Resolving Personal Conflict* (Grand Rapids: Baker, 2004), 40–41. I consider this book a must-read for seminarians and new pastors. In churches that I have served and in the seminary where I now teach, I have found it to be an extraordinary resource for learning the biblical principles of peacemaking and conflict resolution, and an outstanding textbook for adult and youth Sunday school classes, book studies, and leadership training. Peacemaking and conflict resolution are skills that can be learned, and pastors should lead by acquiring, modeling, and teaching them.

11. Presbyterian Church in America, General Assembly, *The Book of*

Church Order of the Presbyterian Church in America, 6th ed. (Lawrenceville, GA: Christian Education and Publication, 2013), 8–3.

12. Rosaria Champagne Butterfield, *Openness Unhindered: Further Thoughts of an Unlikely Convert on Sexual Identity and Union with Christ* (Pittsburgh: Crown and Covenant Publications, 2015), 147.

13. J. C. Ryle, *Practical Religion* (Edinburgh: Banner of Truth, 2013), 324.

14. William S. Plumer, *Psalms: A Critical and Expository Commentary with Doctrinal and Practical Remarks* (Carlisle, PA: Banner of Truth, 1990), 1139.

15. Charles Simeon, *Horae Homileticae*, vol. 18, *Philippians to 1 Timothy* (London: Holdworth and Ball, 1832–36), 283.

16. Charles Bridges, *The Christian Ministry: With an Inquiry into the Causes of Its Inefficiency* (Carlisle, PA: Banner of Truth, 1991), 157.

17. John Owen, *The Works of John Owen*, ed. William H. Goold, vol. 7 (Edinburgh: T&T Clark, n.d.), 190.

18. James S. Stewart, *The Gates of New Life* (New York: Charles Scribner's Sons, 1940), 189.

Index of Scripture

Index of Subjects and Names

THE REFORMED EXPOSITORY COMMENTARY SERIES

The Reformed Expository Commentary is a 30-year project to provide reliable understanding and application of all the books of the Bible.

Each title goes through three different stages of editing—each by a specialist in biblical studies, pastoral application, and editorial rigor. This process ensures high standards for each addition to the series. This quality has been recognized with a prestigious award from *WORLD* magazine.*

Every book in the series is accessible to both pastors and lay readers. Each volume provides exposition that gives careful attention to the biblical text, is doctrinally Reformed, focuses on Christ through the lens of redemptive history, and applies the Bible to our contemporary setting.

RESPECTED PASTORS AND THEOLOGIANS HAVE PRAISED THE SERIES

"Well researched and well reasoned, practical and pastoral, shrewd, solid, and searching." —J. I. Packer

"A rare combination of biblical insight, theological substance, and pastoral application." —R. Albert Mohler Jr.

"Here, rigorous expository methodology, nuanced biblical theology, and pastoral passion combine." —R. Kent Hughes

"This series promises to be both exegetically sensitive and theologically faithful." —Mark Dever

"An invaluable treasure house. . . . A must-read." —Steven J. Lawson

"Those of us who regularly preach need commentaries that provide the best biblical scholarship and that also understand the challenges of today's pastorate. This series ably speaks to both needs." —Bryan Chapell

ADD THE REFORMED EXPOSITORY COMMENTARY TO YOUR LIBRARY

*WORLD magazine's 2017 Series of the Year

DO YOU KNOW YOUR SHEEP?

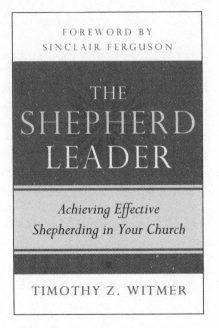

FOREWORD BY
SINCLAIR FERGUSON

THE
SHEPHERD
LEADER

*Achieving Effective
Shepherding in Your Church*

TIMOTHY Z. WITMER

Leaders in the church are called to be shepherds, not a board of directors. This requires involvement in a personal shepherding ministry among the people. *The Shepherd Leader* unpacks the four primary ministries of shepherds—knowing, feeding, leading, and protecting—on macro (churchwide) and micro (personal) levels, providing seven elements to be incorporated into an effective shepherding plan.

"I read Witmer's book in one sitting. I found it that engaging and helpful. This is 'practical theology' at its best: applying biblical principles to contemporary pastoral needs. . . . If you can read this book and not be motivated to develop a more effective shepherding ministry in your church, you might want to check if you are called to shepherd in the first place." **—Kevin DeYoung**

"WHAT WAS THAT SERMON ABOUT?"

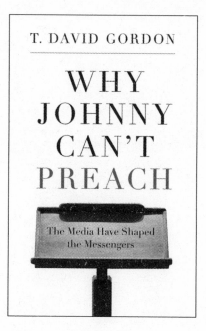

T. David Gordon has identified a problem, one that affects us all and needs fixing. Our preaching is just not communicating properly anymore. Fortunately, Gordon refuses to stand by and watch—and we should too. In this short book, he provides a concise, in-depth look at the causes of this failure and also shows us how to make things better.

"While there are helpful studies of popular culture and important books on proper biblical interpretation and theology, this book does both. I couldn't help but wince as I recognized myself in Gordon's descriptions, but he writes so clearly and convincingly that I couldn't help but be grateful. *Why Johnny Can't Preach* should be read by anyone who cares about preaching." —**Michael Horton**